NOVEMBER:
THE CRUELEST MONTH
GREAT LAKES
WRECKS

FREDERICK STONEHOUSE

Avery Color Studios, Inc.
Gwinn, Michigan

© 2010 Avery Color Studios, Inc.

ISBN: 978-1-892384-55-3

Library of Congress Control Number: 2010902555

First Edition–2010

10   9   8   7   6   5   4   3

Published by Avery Color Studios, Inc.
Gwinn, Michigan 49841

Cover photo: the *Algoma*, Rutherford B. Hayes Library

TABLE OF CONTENTS

NOVEMBER IS THE
CRUELEST MONTH

There are different ways to say the same thing; the, "Witch of November" or "Gales of November" being common phrases speaking to the huge number of Great Lakes ships wrecked in November. Let there be no doubt - November is the "big guerilla" for Great Lakes shipwrecks, chewing up good ships and crews with a ravenous appetite. Even modern freighters today take care when the lakes turn ugly in November.

Certainly the Lakes' most famous shipwrecks occurred in this most dangerous of months. The *Edmund Fitzgerald*, *Carl D. Bradley* and *Daniel J. Morrell* being most prominent among a very long list of disasters.

The tragedies of the Great Storm in 1913, November gales in 1905 and infamous losses in the 1940 Armistice Day Storm all eloquently echo the cruelty of November as do a host of other calamities.

We all too often think of shipwreck only terms of the loss of ships with perhaps a passing reference to the number of crew killed as almost an afterthought. To a degree this is backward since it is the human tragedy that really is paramount. When the schooner *W.W. Arnold* wrecked on Lake Superior's Shipwreck Coast all souls aboard perished with her. Other than the captain's name, the others are for practical purposes, unknown. What about their mothers and fathers, wives, children and even friends? How did the terrible shipwreck affect them? In a way their stories are an extension of the wreck and are sadly stories rarely told. Historians estimate roughly 30,000 people lost their lives in Great Lakes shipwrecks. Without making any estimate of how many folks were affected by each death, it is easy to see the number must be huge and the potential impact to others staggering.

Why there are so many losses in November is essentially two-fold. Traditionally November was the last month for shipping. In the early days vessel insurance ended on December 1, so the prudent vessel owner made his last push while his ship was still "covered." When technology improved and vessels became safer, thus extending the season somewhat, November was still the month crowded with end of season shipping.

Given the propensity for November storms, the end of season ships became targets for wind and wave.

In the fall of the year cold, dry air rolling south from northern Canada, converges with warm, moist air coming north from the Gulf of Mexico, which in turn form large storm systems in the middle of the North American continent. Sometimes several such systems move along similar routes toward the Great Lakes. When the cold air reaches the lakes it is warmed by the water thus the disturbance gains strength, spawning the infamous gales of November.

Looking at it a little differently, in November two storm tracks typically converge over the Lakes; one coming southeastward from Alberta and the other from the lee of the central Rocky Mountains northeast toward the Lakes. When a cyclonic system moves over the lakes, its power is intensified by the jet stream above and the warm waters below allowing the storm to maintain hurricane-force winds up to 100 mph and pile up waves over 50 feet as well as drop several feet of snow or inches of rain. These powerful storms can remain over the Great Lakes for days, constantly fed by the comparatively warm water.

The loss of a ship is only a material disaster but the death of so many sailors and passengers is a tragedy of major dimensions. The number of ships lost to November storms is generally known, the terrible toll of people less so.

November truly is the "cruelest month."

W.W. ARNOLD -
A LONELY PLACE TO DIE

Certainly one of the worst Lake Superior shipwrecks in terms of human suffering was that of the schooner *W.W. Arnold*. The two-masted, 426-ton schooner hauled out of Marquette bound for Cleveland with ore at 4:00 p.m. on November 4, 1869. Under command of Captain Beardsley, she carried two passengers and a crew of eight or nine sailors.

About four hours after the *Arnold* left the ore dock, a "great gale of wind" accompanied by blinding snow roared down from the northwest blasting the city. The storm raged for 24 hours producing extremely high seas sending pounding waves high over the breakwater and straining lines of ships safely moored. Lightkeeper Edward Ashman at Whitefish Point remembered it as the most terrific storm he had ever seen. And Whitefish Point is notorious for receiving the business end of Superior's worst gaggers!

Regardless of the intensity of the storm little concern was initially felt for the *Arnold*, even when word came back to town she hadn't reached the Soo. Marine men thought she was too well built and her captain too experienced to have serious problems. Likely she just tucked in somewhere to wait out the worst of the blow. Some men opined she made it past Whitefish Point and was laying in shelter off Batchawana on the Canadian coast, but as the days passed and nothing was heard from her, folks knew something serious happened.

Marquette ore docks circa 1873. At the time Marquette was the premier port on Lake Superior. Author Collection

Vessels arriving in Marquette from the Soo had no word of her whereabouts. They found no floating wreckage field or saw anything untoward along the shore. She was just "gone."

A long month passed, the schooner having dropped through a "crack in the lake." On December 7, an Indian mail carrier arrived in Munising with news he found a wreck on the beach at the mouth of the Two-Heart River approximately 90 miles to the east. More ominously, a local Indian trapper told him he counted ten bodies scattered along the water's edge! Neither Indian would approach closer to the wreck, apparently overawed by the fear of encountering ghosts, at least according to contemporary news accounts. In their defense the desolate stretch of coast is indeed a spooky place, bereft of humans and the rightful domain of wolves and other creatures of the deep forest.

The intrepid mail carriers (some Indian, some Meti and a few renegade French-Canadians) were virtually the only way to keep communication open during the frigid Lake Superior winters. With ice choking the lake and the storm gods raging wild, vessel traffic stopped completely, usually by the end of November, not to resume

Whitefish Point Light marked a critical turning point for upbound and downbound vessels. Both it and Copper Harbor light were placed in service in 1849, the oldest beacons on Lake Superior. Author Collection

until the ice left sometime in May. On occasion the ice remained until June. It is easy to see how important these dogsled mailmen were to the early pioneers. One observer commented in 1860 that mail carrier, "Frechette passed up the shore with his dog-train to Grand Marais and down again for the Sault (sic Soo). We saw great dogs seated on their haunches baying deep and dismal tones. These animals worked in sleds during the winter. They are large sinewy brutes, of great strength and endurance. Frechette makes the run with them from Grand Marais to the Sault (sic Soo) in two days."

Munising, from the Ojibwa word "Kitchi-Minising" meaning "place of the island," is about 35 miles east of Marquette. The original settlement in the area was on Grand Island where as late as the 1840s a small fur trading post operated. With the discovery of iron on the Marquette Range in 1844 and opening of the Soo locks in 1855, commerce on Superior boomed and increasing attention was paid to Grand Island Harbor as a potential port, especially as a location for smelting iron ore using charcoal burned from the local hardwood forests. To this end, a furnace was established in 1867 near the present city. It only operated for a short nine years but is in part why Munising became Munising.

On December 8, the day after the news reached Munising about the wreckage at the Two-Heart, a quickly organized party of four Munising men left for the site. The difficult journey was apparently undertaken for two reasons. First, Captain Beardsley took several cargoes to Munising with the schooner *Fontanelle* the previous year and made numerous friends in the small settlement. Second, Beardsley was also a Mason in good standing at his Cleveland lodge. Three of the four men in the Munising search party were also Masons so it can be reasoned they were motivated by helping a brother in distress. Such fraternal associations were taken far more seriously during this period of history than they are now.

The group departed Munising in a small boat intending to coast along the Pictured Rocks to Grand Marais, 35 miles to the east, on the first day. The Two-Heart was another 25 miles beyond. But stormy weather forced them to land at the Miners River for the night. The spectacular Pictured Rocks run for 20-odd miles along the coast and in places soar to in excess of 200-feet high. The cliffs are utterly

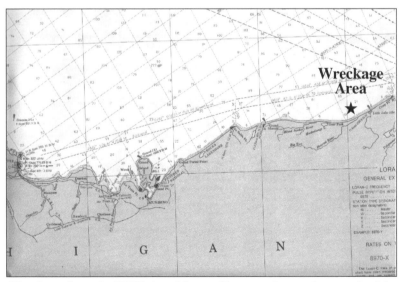

Wreckage from the W.W. Arnold *was discovered near the mouth of the Two-Heart River. Author Collection*

unforgiving in heavy weather, with waves pounding into them in spectacular fashion, sending sheets of spray perhaps 50 feet into the air. The following day, the searchers left their boat ashore and strapped on snowshoes and hiked overland, reaching Grand Marais at dusk after two more nights of camping in the woods.

Grand Marais is steeped in Great Lakes history. The first Europeans to visit were reportedly Frenchman Pierre Esprit Radisson and his companion Sieur du Groseilliers in 1658. Although Grand Marais loosely translates as "great marsh," the harbor was two miles long and an excellent refuge for travelers on the stormy lake. Over the next two centuries, Radisson and Groseilliers were followed by missionaries of various persuasions, voyageurs, lumbermen, fishermen and others seeking to exploit the new frontier. By 1869 settlement at Grand Marais was still sparse, mostly fur trappers and fishermen trying to squeeze a marginal living from an unforgiving land and lake.

At Grand Marais the searchers found welcome shelter at a small trapper's cabin for the night. The next morning they intended to hike the beach to the wreck site but after tramping seven miles found an abandoned fisherman's skiff on the beach. Hastily caulking it and chopping out rough oars from the forest, they continued on by water. It wasn't long before their quick caulking let loose and all hands had to use their jack knives to force rope and handkerchiefs into the gaping seams to keep the skiff afloat. Although they had to bail constantly, they kept going eastward. It was faster than hiking the sandy beach. About nightfall they found a gap in the icebergs jamming together along the shore and landed for the night, camping in the deep woods behind the dunes.

They awoke to Lake Superior roiled by a hard north wind and since it was too rough to launch their small hastily patched skiff through the breakers, they threw their packs on their backs and continued on foot towards the Two-Heart River now six miles distant. After an hour they began to find evidence of the wreck including clothing and canvas scattered on the beach.

They reached what was left of the *Arnold* about 11:00 a.m. on December 11. Considering all the newspaper stories about how strong and well built she was they expected to find her largely intact. Instead, she was "literally torn to atoms" and a "mass of splinters" cast high on the beach. But there was no doubt the wreckage was the *Arnold* since one of the men found her name on a section of bulwark. The men searched for the reported bodies until 4:00 p.m. when a threatening snowstorm forced them to leave, retracing their long journey back to Munising. They reluctantly concluded locating human remains would have to wait until the ice and snow melted in the spring, although it was possible some at least were already devoured or dragged off into the deep woods by local wolves.

They did find a section of her bottom, with some iron ore still in it, a third of a mile west of the river mouth and part of her forward bulwarks on the beach east of the river. The roof of the deck house as well as boxes, chairs, bedding and her smashed yawl were discovered on top of 40-foot high sand banks opposite the main wreckage field.

The following April some of the original search party returned to the wreck and salvaged a quantity of rigging and hardware for the insurance company but it was precious little material. They also discovered the remains of the captain half buried in the beach near the water line about four miles east of the river. When they dug the body out, they found the hands gone and face so decomposed to be unrecognizable. It was only from his general features, as well as the items in his pockets including a bill for ship's stores, they concluded it was Beardsley. He was carefully buried on higher ground. The body of an unidentified sailor was also found near the wreck and interred behind the tree line.

The actual cause of loss was never determined. When one of the search parties discovered her foremast had broken 20-feet above the deck and the jaws of the boom showed evidence of having been chopped with an axe, the disaster was blamed on the broken mast. Without the foremast the schooner would have been helpless in the storm. If the broken foremast was dragging overboard, still connected to the schooner by running and standing rigging and boom, chopping the whole mess clear was vital to any chance of survival. Driven by the towering seas and buffeted by the blasting wind, she must have driven up on the bar off the Two-Heart and gone to pieces very quickly. Since the original search party discovered canvas from her sails three miles from the wreck, it was likely many of her sails were shredded offshore, leaving her largely under bare poles when she hit the bar. Regardless, none of the men would have had a chance of surviving.

It is chilling to think about the horror the men aboard the *Arnold* must have felt. Helpless in the maw of an unholy Superior stem-winder, the captain could only try to keep going eastward and the potential shelter of Whitefish Bay and to get there, he had to stay off the dreaded wave-pounded lee shore. Huge seas smashed into the schooner and blasts of icy wind tore at the little canvas still intact. Crewmen worked the bilge pumps constantly to empty not only water flooding below from the waves but likely also that entering through "spit" caulking.

At some point a crewman must have yelled, "Breakers, breakers ahead," moments before she smashed into the sand bar off the Two-Heart. The impact could have dismasted her, sending one or more of her sticks over the side or at least damaging enough of the standing rigging, it became only a matter of time before they succumbed to the tearing wind and tumbling into the pounding lake. Or perhaps the masts went over long before.

With the ship breaking up beneath them, the crew was faced with the devil's choice. Staying aboard meant near certain death, either from drowning as she came apart or if by some miracle she held together and the storm blew it self out, freezing to death. If they tried for the shore there was a bare chance of survival.

Perhaps some stayed aboard and when the ship shattered in the hammering seas were swept to shore drowning on the way in. Other crewmen may have decided to try to reach the beach by swimming or holding on to floating wreckage. In all likelihood they succumbed to the cold and storm tossed seas before reaching shore.

But if, and it is a very big IF, a sailor reached shore alive what was he to do? There was no shelter of any kind. No settlement, abandoned cabins or people. Just an absolutely desolate beach! If he had dry matches and the energy to climb over the sand, snow and ice to the woods behind the dunes, maybe he could find enough dry tinder to start a fire for life giving warmth. But then what? He still had no shelter, food or hope of rescue! The fire just prolonged death. The agony of living would last just a little longer.

The *Arnold*, owned by Captain J.D. Bothwell of Cleveland, was nearly new, having been built at Buffalo in 1965. Rated A-1 by Lloyds, she was a loss of $19,000 for the vessel and $30,000 in cargo. Of course there was no monetary value assigned to the men.

NOVEMBER: THE CRUELEST MONTH

Like most working vessels the *Arnold* had her share of accidents. In October 1863, she was damaged in collision on the St. Clair Flats. It was very odd how it came about. About 6:30 on a quiet Sunday morning, the tug *Zouave* was towing the schooners. *W.W. Arnold*, *A.J. Rich* and *Clayton Belle* down the St. Clair Flats. Lake St. Clair, about 20 miles across, connects the St. Clair River and the Detroit River. The lake is notoriously shallow (thus the moniker "St. Clair Flats") and although a narrow shipping channel is maintained, the most expeditious way for sailing vessels to transit is by tow.

In any event, the *Arnold* wandered out of the channel and went aground, which brought her to a sudden standstill causing the trailing *Rich* to smash into her stern with great force; completely staving in the *Arnold's* stern, besides breaking off her wheel and two deck beams. The damage was so extensive an entirely new stern was needed. Meantime, the *Clayton Belle* collided in turn with the *Rich*, breaking her stern into atoms, and also destroying her two small boats. Running behind the *Zouave's* string was the tug *Dispatch* with three more schooners. The mayhem ahead caused the *Dispatch* to veer and schooner *Nabob* went aground and was quickly struck by the schooner towed aft suffering considerable damage. All told it was estimated $5,000 was needed to put things right for the damaged *Arnold*.

Three years later, the *Arnold* suffered additional damages in the very restrictive channels in the flats colliding with the schooner *E. Kanter*. On November 4, 1867, she ran around near the Buffalo breakwater due to low water. In May 1869, she damaged her rudder working through spring ice in Escanaba. There is no indication previous damage played any role in her ultimate loss.

The wreck of the *Arnold* had a major emotional impact on Lake Superior residents. One T. Meads penned a poem, "The Wreck of the *Arnold*," in 1870 telling the mournful tale of the wreck:

> "In the beautiful bay of Marquette there lay
> A vessel well built and sound
> That captain is a worthy seaman they say
> As any that could be found

A requiem now we'll sing to the dead
Drowned in the freshwater sea
Praying that each one's soul hath fled
To rest in eternity."

References:

A.B. Bibb, "Life-Saving on the Great Lakes," *Frank Leslie's Popular Monthly, XIII*, April 1882, 396-398.

Buffalo Commercial Advertiser. January 20, 1864; February 26, November 4, 1867.

James L. Carter, *Voyageur's Harbor*, (Grand Marais, Michigan: Pilot Press), 1967, 2-4.

Cleveland Plain Dealer. November 3, 1863.

Marine Disasters on the Western Lakes During 1869, Capt. J.W. Hall.

Mining Journal (Marquette, Michigan). November 20, December 18, 25, 1869; January 1, 8, April 9, 25, May 14, 1870.

Phyllis L. Tag and Thomas A. Tag, *The Lighthouse Keepers of Lake Superior*, (Dayton: Great Lakes Lighthouse Research), 1998.

W.W. Arnold File, Stonehouse Collection.

SATURN AND JUPITER -
WHEN THE PLANETS DIED

The "Big Lake" has never been thought to be hospitable to November sailings although in fact most certainly go without a hitch. Perhaps some foul weather boils over Superior just to make the trip interesting, but usually not more. The reputation for November storms is often worse than it's bite but not always. When the "Witch of November" comes calling, it is often to collect a delinquent account!

Early on the morning of November 27, 1872, the sidewheeler *John A. Dix* pulled out of Marquette hauling the schooner-barges *Saturn* and *Jupiter*. All were heavily loaded with Marquette Range iron ore. Using a steamer to tow old schooners as makeshift barges was an efficient way to move bulk cargos, especially iron ore.

Throughout the day the weather continued to deteriorate and by 5:00 p.m. off Vermilion Point, about 105 miles east of Marquette, a strong north gale overtook them and they were soon laboring heavily in the rolling seas. Half an hour later the towing hawser to the *Jupiter* broke and an hour afterward, the *Saturn* was loose too. In the black and storm blown night it was impossible for the *Dix* to reconnect the tow so she left them to their own devices and ran for shelter behind Whitefish Point. Making the storm even worse, the temperatures plummeted to near zero and the crews on the *Jupiter* and *Saturn* suffered terribly. At least the men on the *Dix* had the heat from her big boiler to huddle around. But on the schooner-barges all they had was the small cook's stove in the galley and perhaps a diminutive "Charley Noble" in the foc'sle. Given the violent motion of the schooners in the storm, firing up either stove may have been problematic. In the parlance of the time, "it was colder than a witch's heart!"

When morning finally broke, the crew of the *Dix* found her deck and upper works covered with nearly a foot of heavy ice. Instead of looking for her missing tows, the *Dix* hauled anchor and steamed on for the Soo. She literally abandoned them to their fate.

There is a story told the steamer's crew implored Captain Joseph Waltman of the *Dix* to return and look for the pair but he refused. Once they moored at the Soo, her angry sailors spread the word about the captain's cowardice and soon local citizens threatened to march on the ship and hoist him up the yardarm by a rope necktie. He fled the ship and escaped into the deep woods with the aid of a local Indian guide. Whether this is all nothing but a tall tale or contains a thread of truth is questionable. That said, there is no record of the *Dix* searching for the *Saturn* or *Jupiter*. She simply abandoned them and their crews. Considering there was every possibility of either ship surviving the storm at best or some of the crewmen making it to the beach if the ships ended up in the breakers, aid from the *Dix* would have been critical for survival, especially along such a desolate coast in the frigid weather.

What happened to the two tows was a mystery soon solved. The *Saturn* was later found aground on the outer bar three miles west of Whitefish Point and the *Jupiter* 12 miles west of her, near the mouth of the Two-Heart River. All those aboard both vessels, 14 men and a woman cook, perished.

The first seaman to see what happened to the pair was the captain of the upbound steamer *China* who spotted first the *Saturn* and then the *Jupiter* an hour or so later. He relayed the sighting to the folks in Marquette as soon as he arrived. Initially reports claimed the hulls of both vessels were visible but later accounts verified only the masts still projected above the waves. Perhaps the hulls were visible when the vessels were firm on the outer sandbars but disappeared in the deeper water between bar and land when blasted off the bar by the thundering seas.

Supposedly only one body was ever officially recovered from the wrecks. Two local Whitefish Point men, John and Jim Clarke, found a sailor frozen stiff, sitting on a log on the beach opposite the *Saturn* wreck. They buried him in a nearby sandbank on the edge of the forest. As the bank gradually eroded they reputedly "moved" him inland several times.

The *Jupiter* was a loss of $12,000 and *Saturn* $13,000. Both ships were owned by Eber B. Ward of Detroit. Captain Peter Howard mastered the *Jupiter* and Dick Stringleman, the *Saturn*.

The losses of the *Arnold*, *Saturn* and *Jupiter* became part of the rational for establishing U.S. Life-Saving Stations along the infamous "Shipwreck Coast," a 50 mile long stretch of barren shore running from Grand Marais east to Whitefish Point. Perhaps a hundred vessels were lost on or off the barren shore. Even today the wooden bones of wrecks can be found along the open beach as well as in the deep off-shore depths. The Board of Lake Underwriters immediately agitated with the Treasury Department to establish Life-Saving Stations along the infamous shore with the result that four stations were established in 1877; Deer Park, Two Heart, Crisp's Point and Vermilion Point. They were the first stations on the Superior and sorely needed. Grand Marais was added in 1901.

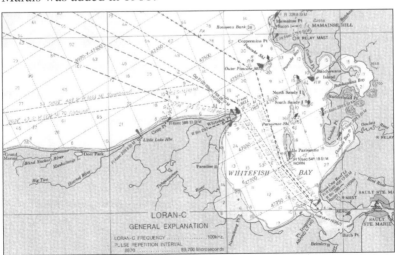

The Saturn *and* Jupiter *disasters provided impetus to establishing Life-Saving Service stations at Deer Park, Crisp's Point, Vermilion Point and Two-Heart River. Author Collection*

NOVEMBER: THE CRUELEST MONTH

The *Dix* was a former Revenue Cutter built in Newburgh, New York in 1865. She was typically stationed in Sault Ste. Marie during the navigation season, wintering in Detroit. She was sold in June 1872, as surplus to a commercial operator.

The storm was a real rip'snorter, some old timers claiming it was the worst they ever experienced. Several ships were badly knocked about. The schooner *Golden Rule* had every inch of canvas blown out and she drifted for a day before bumping ashore in the lower reaches of Whitefish Bay. Her crew was badly frozen. The extreme cold iced several steamers in the St. Marys River and closed the Soo Locks.

The same fierce storm that destroyed the *Jupiter* and *Saturn* also overwhelmed the 354-ton schooner *Charles C. Griswold*. She was downbound with grain when she disappeared with all hands off Gros Cap on the Canadian shore. Since schooner masts were seen projecting from the water nearby it was presumed her point of loss. Built in 1854 in Vermilion, Ohio, she was a loss of $27,000 plus the crew of six.

The 140-foot schooner *William O. Brown* fared lightly better. Also downbound with grain, she went to pieces when the powerful windblasts drove her hard ashore on Point Maimanse, on the Canadian shore northeast of Whitefish Point. Six of her nine-man crew survived but only after a long and difficult overland trek to the Soo.

References:

Donald L. Cannery, *U.S. Coast Guard and Revenue Cutters, 1790-1935*. (Annapolis: U.S. Naval Institute Press, 1995), 35.

Charles C. Griswold, *www.boatnerd.com*.

Chicago Tribune. January 30, 1873.

Janice H. Gerred. "*Saturn* and *Jupiter* Destroyed by Superior," *People and Places, Great Lakes Gazette*, March 10, 1975, 7.

Marquette Mining Journal. December 7, 21, 28, 1872.

Runge Collection, Milwaukee Marine Society.

Wells List, Stonehouse Collection.

H.C. AKELEY -
THREE FOR THE BOTTOM

Sometimes shipwreck is a simple affair. A ship underway on the open lake, a violent storm overtakes her, shake well, throw in a few boarding seas and loose hatch covers and "voila" a shipwreck is born! Others can be far more complicated affairs. The *H.C. Akeley* is a case in point.

The tale starts with the small 100-foot two-masted schooner *Arab* heavily laden with lumber. Foul weather blew her on the beach near St. Joseph, Michigan, on October 31, 1883. She was an old wind-wagon, built in 1854 in Buffalo, and such accidents were not uncommon. Hauled off her sandy perch, she was dragged into the St. Joe harbor and a hole in the hull temporarily patched. Doubtless her seams could use a good caulking too, but that wasn't on the "punch list." Regardless, the captain brought a couple of big steam pumps aboard with an engineer to operate them. One pump should be enough to keep any leaking in check and the second was really insurance against additional leaks or pump failure. Pumps weren't all that reliable and a second one was very good planning.

Early in the evening of November 10, the 77-foot tug *Protection* took her in tow and headed outbound for Racine, Wisconsin. The tug was only 10 years old and fully capable of handling the small *Arab*. Owned by the Vessel Owners Towing Company of Chicago, she was rebuilt only the year before. Aboard the tug were a captain, mate, steward, three seamen and two engineers for a total of eight people. Two firemen were added to the schooner strictly to run the pumps.

The lake was described as, "calm and splendid" as the pair plowed their way across on a northwesterly course. At 4:00 a.m., when they were about in mid-lake, the tug crew suddenly heard yelling from astern. The *Arab* was only about 500 feet back and they watched the crew running aft as the schooner rolled slowly to starboard, sinking by the head in a nearly perpendicular position. Within what seems like mere seconds only ten feet or so of the *Arab's* portside stern quarter was showing and the crew desperately hanging on to it.

On later investigation it turns out while only one steam pump

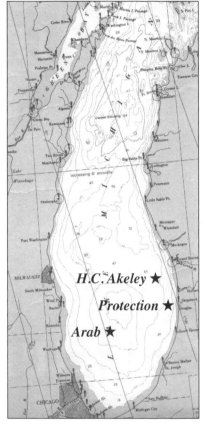

was needed to keep her clear, the second pump was kept ready but not running. When the working pump started not working, the engineers tried to fire up the second pump but the water flooded so fast it gave the schooner a sharp bow down position and since both heavy pumps were forward, their great weight contributed to the rapidly growing angle.

Remember the two pumps were <u>steam</u> pumps and needed a head of steam to run. And it takes a while, perhaps a good 45 minutes, to build enough steam pressure in a cold boiler to run a pump. The engineers tried to fire the spare pump up as quickly as possible but it was longer than the *Arab* had afloat.

Tragically one of the engineers drowned when she rolled, witnesses claiming he was standing forward when she took a saddened lurch and the siding pump smashed into him, trapping him aboard.

H.C. AKELEY - THREE FOR THE BOTTOM

The mate on the *Protection* reacted to the disaster by immediately ringing stop on the engine room telegraph and then astern to back down to pick up the schooner's sailors. However, the propeller caught the towline swathing it in a massive knot of manila, stopping the engine cold!

Although their ship was dead in the water, the tug's sailors quickly launched a small boat, rescuing the schooner sailors. Soon after the *Arab* crew climbed aboard the tug, the old schooner dove for the bottom and soon was looking at the lake from the wrong side! The tug men saved them just in time.

What had to this point been very good weather for November now started to go to hell. The wind began to blow with increasing force, the seas building to higher and higher peaks. Knowing it was vital to clear the propeller as quickly as possible, the tug men worked hard to do just that. For four long hours they cut, pulled and swore every blue oath in the book in an effort to unsnarl the propeller. Alone and in pairs, men were tied off with safety lines as they hung in water astern trying to clear the hawser. Little if any progress was made.

About 10:00 a.m. the men gave up. The lake was firmly in the grasp of a northwest gale and getting anything accomplished on the small tug was impossible. In spite of the wind and seas, the tug rode well, laying with her bow to, quartering into the breakers.

An hour later the wooden 230-foot steamer *H.C. Akeley*, bound from Chicago for Buffalo with a cargo of 54,000 bushels of corn, arrived on the scene. Signaled by the tug's whistle, the steamer approached and was made aware of her trouble. After a little negotiation she put a hawser on the tug and continued on her course for the Manitou Passage with the *Protection* following obediently along behind. A fat and unexpected towing fee brightened the otherwise gale-lashed day for her captain.

By afternoon the wind was blowing a powerful gale and the weather bureau in Grand Haven was clocking windblasts at 52 mph, the wind building a terrific sea and the *Akeley* was having a very difficult time of it. After a series of especially powerful seas slammed into her, there was load rumble from below as her cargo shifted and she took a pronounced starboard list. Now virtually every wave rolled over her deck. The list combined with the stress of the gale put a tremendous strain on her rudder and about 7:00 p.m., it failed, quickly followed by her engine. Perhaps water flooding below dousing her boiler fire or the engineer fearing a boiler explosion blew off the steam. The crew soon ran up her sails but the blasting winds soon shredded the canvas.

All through the long storm blown night the steamer and tug drifted wildly before wind and sea, still tethered by the towing hawser. About 4:00 a.m. one of the steamer's lifeboats washed away into the black night and at 10:00 a.m. her mizzenmast crashed to the deck, smashing the smokestack and remaining lifeboat.

During the afternoon the gale moderated and the tug's crew discovered their propeller was apparently free of the hawser. Perhaps the wash of the waves partially cleared it. Regardless, at 6:00 p.m. she cast loose from the *Akeley* and her captain rang up full ahead to the engineer. He anticipated making port, refueling and running back out and towing the steamer to safety doubtlessly "reversing" the towing charges. Perhaps the so far benighted trip would in the end be profitable. But instead of going ahead as he signaled, the tug could only go in reverse. Giving up the effort he shut down to his engine, steamer and tug drifting together across the lake. Over time the two moved apart, their size difference accounting for different rates of drift.

When dawn slowly broke the next morning a gray streak on the eastern horizon showed the tug coming up on land. Approximately 9:00 a.m., she dropped her anchor about a half-mile off the beach and a mile or so north of Saugatuck.

A succession of sharp blasts from her whistle brought a throng of local residents tumbling out of their warm homes to gawk at the wreck in the offing. The tug was pitching and rolling terribly, one minute visible to the spectators, the next lost to view in the wave trough. The crew stuck an oar upright into the bow with a hunk of torn sail tied on it as an ad hoc distress signal, the canvas blowing iron tight in the ferocious wind. Conditions were far too severe for local fishermen using Mackinac boats to try a rescue so a group of leading citizens sent a telegram to the Life-Saving Station at Grand Haven, 28 miles to the north, asking for help. But the reply dashed their hopes. The crew was already at work on the rescue of the *Clara Parker*, nine miles from the station and unavailable.

Not deterred, another telegram chattered off to the St. Joseph Station, 50 miles to the south. When Keeper William L. Stevens received the message, he immediately tried to contact the District Superintendent at Grand Haven for permission to go to a rescue so far from his station but the man was with the Grand Haven crew and out of touch. Rather than delay waiting for his return, he used his judgment to go where his help was most needed.

A quick reply was wired back to Saugatuck that his crew would leave as soon as possible and to prepare for their arrival. He also arranged for the Chicago and West Michigan Railway to transport them north to Saugatuck.[1] However since the Life-Saving Station was on the wrong side of the St. Joseph River from the train depot, his crew had to transport all their gear, including beach apparatus cart, across the river. This was easier said than done since the storm was sending a barrage of waves up the river threatening to overturn the small private ferry. However they managed to reach the far bank and drag their apparatus to the depot. To their dismay they discovered while the engine was belching black smoke and ready to go, the only car available was a baggage car, not the flatcar they expected. They could have easily tied off the beach apparatus to the flatcar but to use the baggage car the crew had to first load 800 pounds of rescue gear

The beach cart was a critical piece of Life-Saving Service equipment as it was for the Coast Guard through the 1940s. Crews often pulled the 900-pound cart over miles of sandy beaches to get to the scene of a wreck. Author Collection

separately, then disassemble the cart to fit it through the small door. It all took time but was done as quickly as possible. Realizing he still had responsibilities in St. Joseph, Keeper Stevens left his Number One Surfman behind at the station. Should the Life-Savers be needed in the crew's absence, the Number One could organize a volunteer rescue from local marine men if needed using the station's spare equipment.

At 12:55 p.m. the C&WM train started on its 60 mile run north, twisting its way through farmers' fields and thick woods. About three hours later the train wheezed to a stop at the little village of Richmond, on the banks of the Kalamazoo River due east of Saugatuck where the tug *Ganges* was standing by with steam up to transfer them to Saugatuck. After a few minutes of heavy work made lighter by the willing hands of townspeople eager to help, the tug was loaded and churning her way down river. Several times she bottomed in the low water but each time her powerful screw forced her over the shallow spot. Two hours and 13 miles later she arrived at the lighthouse and the Life-Savers quickly unloaded and headed for the wreck.

When they finally arrived opposite the wreck it was clear she was beyond the range of the Lyle gun. Nominal range was 400 yards but in critical conditions a good keeper could nurse another hundred yards if the situation warranted, but only at some risk. All the keepers were very good at getting the maximum effort from their assets, be it equipment or human, or they wouldn't be keepers. But the *Protection* was too far out to even consider a shot. All the men could do was wait for her to drift closer to shore.

At 6:00 p.m. the wind hauled hard northwest and thick snow squalls swept in from the lake. By every indicator the gale showed signs of cranking up again and increasing in violence. The Life-Savers accompanied by the crowd of local citizens waited patiently in the gathering gale for about three hours when the tug's saddened whistle blasts alerted them the anchor was dragging again and she was heading for the breakers.

The crew on the tug figured this was the end. As long as the anchor held they had a chance of riding out the storm but now all bets were off. They shook hands all around and resignedly waited their fate.

The hammering seas were forcing the beleaguered tug southward and Keeper Stevens realized she would come ashore south of the river mouth. Since he and his crew were on the wrong side of the river, they grabbed the towing ropes and dragged the beach apparatus cart to the river where the government tug *Graham* ran them across the gap.

Landing on the south side of the river was difficult in the extreme. A large pond inward of the beach meant the only possible location was on the south pier itself. But the pier was made of cribs, wood compartments perhaps 20-feet square filled with rocks. Moving the wreck cart across the top of the cribs was impossible as there was no plank top to it. The large crowd jumped in and tearing up the planks used for the lightkeeper's walk, decked the cribs over and then hauled the cart over each crib in turn until reaching the beach.

The beach was equally impassible if not worse! It was covered with driftwood of every size and description but the crowd "harnessed up" to the drag ropes and hauled the heavy cart over each obstacle with sheer brute force.

The scene on the beach was between eerie and surreal. The northwest wind and snow swirled hard and fast, Life-Savers and citizens sharply shadowed by the yellow glow of oil lanterns wobbling on the slowly moving cart, dancing flames from bonfires casting bright pools of light reflecting back from the high sand banks behind the beach. Straining men pulling on the harness and staggering in the sand with fatigue. The point they were making for, where the keeper estimated the wreck would strike within gun range, was a bare half mile from the river, but it took nearly an hour of desperate struggle to make that short distance.

Up until this time the men on the tug had no idea the Life-Savers were on the scene. It was too dark to make them out on the beach. But the light from the big bonfires gave enough illumination to see the surfmen and local residents battling their way over the beach with the beach apparatus cart and realize hope was at hand.

About 200 yards off shore the tug slammed into the outer bar with a crash. Immediately huge combers swept over the *Protection*. She continued to rise and fall as wave after wave slammed into her hull. The pilothouse soon smashed into kindling as well as engine room companion way and the lower deck flooded with water. Fireman William Grace, grasping an aft rail, was swept overboard disappearing into the boiling surf.

One of the tug's crew had had enough! He was tired of just waiting to die, tired of drifting around the lake for days, and mostly just tired of waiting for rescue that never came. He tied on a lifejacket and jumped overboard intending to swim ashore himself. Incredibly he did, walking up from the black waves and directly to a beach fire to warm up. A Life-Saver called it, "one chance in a million."

It wasn't long before the pounding waves forced the tug over the bar and into deeper water between bar and beach. Her anchor now took bite and she was at least partially stable although in a sinking condition.

About 10:00 p.m. the tug stopped drifting and the Life-Savers set up the Lyle gun and let her rip, neatly dropping the shotline over the tug. Since it was well after dark, Keeper Stevens had to aim the gun by watching the white flash of waves breaking on the wreck. The first line was swept away by the foaming billows before the crew could grab it but they caught the second line. The whip line was quickly sent out followed by the hawser and breeches buoy.

It was fortunate the Life-Savers shot when they did. A heavy snow squall soon blotted the tug from view completely. The whip and breeches buoy hawser just disappeared into a swirling cloud of frigid white surrounded by the dark night.

The tug was still live, moving when the waves slammed it, the hawser with buoy flexed, drawing tight then dipping into the waves. The Life-Savers constantly adjusted their sand anchor and crotch to keep proper tension on it, but regardless of their efforts, most of the tug's crew ended up being dragged through the water before reaching shore. Luckily a gang of 35-40 local citizens was providing the hauling muscle on the whip as directed by a Life-Saver, so they were pulled so fast Keeper Stevens claimed they left a "streak of foam behind them."

One by one all 15 men aboard were brought to safety on shore. And one by one the frozen victims, their clothing stiff with ice, were bundled off to the beach fires to warm up and given strong stimulants. As soon as everyone was ashore, a dozen of the crew were taken to the tug *Graham* and run up to a hotel at Saugatuck for warm clothing and food. Three of the men were judged too exhausted and cold to survive the trip and instead conveyed to the lighthouse for immediate succor.

The Life-Savers weren't treated as gratefully. Keeper Stevens and two of his crew spent the entire time the men were being brought ashore standing waist deep in the surf helping them to the beach.

When they finally staggered up the beach their clothing was frozen stiff! After packing up their gear the surfmen, now without the help of the long gone civilians, dragged the weighty beach cart back over the debris strewn strand and eventually up to the hotel at Saugatuck, arriving at 2:00 a.m. In all likelihood the warm food was long gone but at least heat was available and a piece of floor to snatch a moment's sleep. They started back to St. Joseph the next afternoon, arriving early in the morning of the 15th. It was just another rescue for the men of the old Life-Saving Service.

Meanwhile far out on the lake the *Akeley* continued to slowly settle in the water. Likely her seams opened in the gale and certainly she took copious amounts of water down her hatches from the seas rolling over her spar deck. It was, in the words of the old sea shanty, "Leave Her, Johnny, Leave Her," time to abandon ship. Unfortunately there was only a single small yawl left aboard. Since the boat could only hold a dozen men at most, the remaining six, including Captain Edwin Strech, Mate John Kingston, a steward, passenger and several deckhands, took their chances on the steamer gambling she would somehow stay afloat long enough for them to cobble together a makeshift raft. It was a bad choice. Shortly after the yawl pulled away, the steamer took the plunge stern first, taking the stay-aboards down with her.

As luck would have it, the schooner *Driver*, under Captain Daniel F. Miller, came booming along and spotting the yawl full of survivors, hove to and brought them aboard. Since the schooner was herself heavily damaged from the gale, Captain Miller demonstrated extraordinary seamanship and courage in rescuing the victims. In fact the feat was so remarkable the Treasury Department awarded him a Gold Life-Saving Medal!

The *Akeley* was built in Grand Haven by Thomas W. Kirby at the Mechanics Dry Dock in 1881. She was named for Healy Cady Akeley, a local businessman who later became a millionaire lumber baron.

NOVEMBER: THE CRUELEST MONTH

References:

Annual Report, U.S. Life-Saving Service 1884, 20-27. NARA RG 26.

Evans E. Kerrigan. *The Sea Shall Not Have Them*. (Norton Heights, Connecticut: Medallic Publishing Company, 1971.) n.p.

New York Times. August 1, 1912.

Jack Sheridan, and Kit Lane. *Storm, Fire and Ice, Shipwrecks of the Saugatuck Area*. (Saugatuck, Michigan: Saugatuck Douglas Historical Society, 2002), n.p.

Stonehouse File - *H.C. Akeley*.

Valerie Olson Van Heest, "Searching for a Steamer," *Michigan History*, July-August 2003, 10-17.

Ditto Van Heest, "A Glimpse Into the Past: The Discovery of the *H.C. Akeley*," *Joint Achieves of Holland Quarterly*, 1-5.

Footnote:

[1]The Chicago and Michigan Railway operated between 1881 and 1899. It was one of the three companies, which merged later to become the Pere Marquette Railway.

ALGOMA -
A DAY OF GLORY, A DAY OF LOSS

The morning of November 7, 1885 dawned bright and prosperous for the Canadian Pacific Railroad. Years of labor were being rewarded by the completion of its first trans-Canada rail link. On that day the last spike was being driven at Craigellachie, British Columbia, finally connecting Canada from Atlantic to Pacific.[1]

The first transcontinental railroad in the U.S. was finished 16 years earlier. Further south on the rugged coast of Isle Royale, another drama was being enacted. The CPR steel steamer *Algoma* with 48 passengers and crew was being destroyed by a vicious Lake Superior gale.[2]

Launched on July 31, 1883, the *Algoma* was a product of the Aitken and Mansel shipyard, Kelvinhaugh, at Whiteinch on the shores of Scotland's Clyde River. Miss Schaw of Glasgow performed the usual naming ceremony to the delight of the assembled crowd. Built especially for the CPR, the new steamer was 1,773 gross tons, 263-feet in length, 38-feet in beam and 23 in depth.

Her fore and aft compound steam engine was supplied by steam from two steel boilers made from steel plate an inch thick. The 1,700 horsepower engine could drive her at a speed of 18 mph turning a propeller 13 and 1/2 foot in diameter. Thirteen other engines were aboard, used for everything from hoisting her anchors and freight, working various pumps and steering gear among other applications.

NOVEMBER: THE CRUELEST MONTH

The CPR steamer Algoma *underway.* Author Collection

As typical her primary wheel was in the pilothouse forward and an emergency aft.

Her design was ultimately well proven evidenced by the long lives of her sisters, the *Alberta* and *Athabasca*, also part of the CPR fleet. All were rated A-1 by Lloyd's, the top rating for new steamers.[3]

The *Alberta* and *Athabasca* had outstanding careers in the CPR fleet. In 1910 the *Athabasca* was taken to Collingwood and lengthened to 298 feet resulting in a tonnage of 2,784. The following year the *Alberta* came out of the yard, even larger, 309 feet and 2,829 gross tons. In 1916 both were relegated to freight only service when it was decided the CPR steamers *Manitoba*, *Keewatin* and *Assiniboia* could handle the full passenger trade. *Alberta* was sold in 1946 to a Chicago firm and scrapped the following year. The same year the *Athabasca* was scrapped in Canada. Their 60-year careers gave powerful testimony to the strong construction of the original design.

When she came out, the *Algoma* had accommodations for 180 first class cabin passengers and 200 in steerage bunks but this could be increased to 1,000 if needed.[4] All the sisters carried six lifeboats (yawlboats) and roughly 600 life jackets. Each boat had a compass, bucket for bailing and a sail rig. No mention was made of the capacity of the boats but clearly it wasn't sufficient for anything approaching a normal passenger load. But a steel ship with six watertight compartments was unsinkable, right?

The Algoma's *sistership* Alberta *in Owen Sound, the eastern terminus of the line. Author Collection*

The *Alberta* was built by Connell and Company, Whiteinch, and launched July 12 and *Athabasca* by Aitken and Mansel on July 3. The three ships were first CPR ships, well before the company became involved in saltwater shipping. They were also the first large steel passenger ships on the Lakes. All three also carried fore and mizzen-masts as well as fore staysail so the press of canvas could supplement the power of their mighty Scottish steam engine.

They were built in Scotland because of political considerations. At the time Canada had no shipyards capable of constructing steel vessels and it was considered unthinkable to have them built in the United States. The only other option was in Britain and that meant Scotland. The Scots were fine shipbuilders with a stellar reputation and having the three sisters built there would add a spot of prestige to the CPR line. All were thought practically unsinkable and were valued at $325,000.

NOVEMBER: THE CRUELEST MONTH

The Athabasca *in Owen Sound. Author Collection*

The triplets also were reputedly the first passenger vessels on the Great Lakes with electric lights. Reportly not a single oil lantern or even a match was allowed on any of them. The electric work was provided by the Canadian Edison Electric Company of Hamilton. An Edison dynamotor powered 110 lights, each a 16-candlepower unit. A lamp with a "flexible conductor" was a special feature of the installation. Today we would call it a work light but it was cutting edge stuff in 1884. Even the stoves in the galley were all electric as were the "cigar lighters."

Hot and cold running water was provided throughout the ships, including steerage. Additional water piping was provided in various locations for fire fighting use and the holds had steam piping with release nozzles, too. In the event of fire the engineers could damp the blaze out with live steam. It was claimed 50 psi was constantly maintained in the pipes to allow an instant response to fire. The only part of the ships not made of steel were the upper decks and, of course, cargo.

The *Algoma's* first real trip other than her builder's trial was the trans-Atlantic crossing from her Scottish yard to the mouth of the St. Lawrence River. As with most ships being delivered, she didn't travel empty but carried a profitable cargo.

The *Athabasca* departed Scotland first on August 23 but returned shortly with a leaky boiler problem. Quickly fixed, she left a second time on September 1, arriving at Montreal on the 23rd. *Alberta* departed on September 10 but waited for the *Algoma* at the Tail of the Bank, an anchorage in the upper Firth of Clyde. The area got it's name from a sandbar immediately to the east. It was a popular point of embarkation for many immigrants to Canada and the U.S. The *Algoma* met the *Alberta* on the 24th and both arrived at Quebec on October 8.

The crossing was uneventful and in all respects the *Algoma* behaved as the champion she was. At Montreal she was cut in two and thus disfigured, towed through the short St. Lawrence canals, Lake Ontario and the Welland Canal to Buffalo where she was reassembled like her sisters at the Union Drydock Company yard. They were "cut" by knocking the heads off the rivets at the appropriate plate joints. Since they were specially built to accommodate the halving it was smoothly accomplished. The

Note the ornate scrolling around the stern of the Athabasca. *Author Collection*

watertight bulkheads on either side of the cut were so well built they served to float the sections during her "half" trip without additional coffer damning although camels were used to level out the stern.[5]

Once they were assembled at Buffalo all continued west under their own steam to Port Colborne for some additional fitting out. When the three left Scotland while seaworthy, they were far from finished. There was a complete absence of cabins on the upper deck other than a very makeshift pilothouse. At Port Colborne the ship

The Athabasca *laying up a dock. Author Collection*

The well appointed smoking salon of the Athabasca. *Author Collection*

carpenters went to work building a long wood cabin on the upper deck. It was essentially a long gallery with staterooms on either side. This was the only deck with passenger accommodations and the resulting individual quarters were certainly minimal but superior to those on earlier vessels. There was no separate dining salon so tables were just arranged down the middle of the gallery. The roof of the gallery also served as an outside observation deck. The pilothouse forward was very small and low. An old fashioned open bridge was on top.

The ships were painted black with comparatively high boot tops or band of paint running along the waterline. A narrow band of white paint ran the length of the ships just below the deck level. Cabins

The dining salon of the *Athabasca*. Note the passenger cabins on both sides as well as the ornate accompaniments. *Author Collection*

were painted white and the funnel black with a wide red band midway up with a narrow white band within.

When the fitting out was finished it was on to Owen Sound on Georgian Bay where their arrival sparked great interest. Everyone was looking forward to seeing the much anticipated new steamers. The *Algoma* arrived on May 10, *Alberta* on the 11th and *Athabasca* on the 13th.

The local paper proclaimed: "No such vessels have ever been seen on the Great Lakes but their excellence lies not in the gorgeousness of their furniture or the gingerbread work of decoration but in their superiority over all other lake craft in model construction and equipment…"

The first arrival of the *Algoma* in Port Arthur was a major event. No one had ever seen a steamer like her before and there were THREE of them! It was claimed 800 to 1,000 people crowded down to the docks to take a good look at her. Considering she carried over 1,000 passengers ready to disembark, it was a massive gathering of

Note the painted boot top, white cabins, white stripe beneath the rail and white stripe on the funnel. Her sails are furled but ready for use.
Author Collection

humanity for the town. There was some fear the dock would collapse from the weight and barriers were erected to keep things under a modicum of control.

Although built from a proven design the *Algoma*, as did her sisters, carried a novel innovation - a Plimsoll mark. The Plimsoll mark is painted on the hull of a vessel to indicate how heavily (and thus safely loaded) a ship is. The *Algoma* and her sisters may have been the first vessels on the Great Lakes to be so marked. The marks looked like small circles with bars painted across them. The British Board of Trade had recently adopted them and its use was made mandatory by an Act of Parliament. Samuel Plimsoll was a Member of Parliament known as the "Sailor's Friend" for his work improving maritime safety, invariably against the active and vehement resistance of British ship owners.

The *Algoma* began her Lakes career on May 11, 1884, carrying a load of roughly 1,100 passengers, mostly Brits and Swedes and CPR supplies from Owen Sound on Lake Huron to Port Arthur, Lake

All of the sisters were very popular with the traveling public. Author Collection

Superior. This was more people than she was intended to carry but the great majority were in "steerage" class. The demand to move west was great and the CPR worked hard to meet it. The *Alberta* left Owen Sound on May 13 and *Athabasca* on May 15. The scheduled trip took up two days with the sisters departing Owen Sound on Tuesday, Thursday and Saturday, arriving at Port Arthur on Thursday, Saturday and Monday. The ships were filling in the middle part of the still unfinished transcontinental rail line. The link from the Atlantic to Owen Sound was finished as was the Port Arthur west portion but the run north of Lake Superior was still under construction.

The three sisters were closely integrated with the rail schedule. Passengers could leave Toronto at 10:45 a.m., reach Owen Sound at 3:05 p.m. and depart on one of the sisters at 4:00 p.m. There wasn't a lot of wasted time! The Owen Sound rail station was on the dock just steps from the gangway to the steamers.

Travelers were accommodated in five classes. If first or tourist, they received meals and a berth in one of the 58 staterooms, generally with upper and lower berths and a convertible sofa. Second, Colonist and Immigrant classes were only provided with room on the main deck, including a berth but not bedding or meals.

First class meals were said to be very good although not high cuisine. One passenger complained there were too many dishes offered! Over time the sisters developed a reputation for less variety

The Algoma *waiting to enter the Weitzel Lock in the Soo.* Author Collection

but larger quantities and especially good fresh baked pies and fish. Many travelers just thought of the food as good, solid Canadian fare.

The *Algoma, Athabasca* and *Alberta* soon were an integral part of the CPR system providing a vital connection between the Owen Sound railhead and the one at Port Arthur. As grain was a major item handled by the CPR, the three sisters often carried grain from the Port Arthur elevators to those at Owen Sound.

Building the trans-Canada rail link was an extremely difficult job. Not only did roadbeds have to be blasted through the Rockies but various challenges of the region north of Lake Superior had to be overcome. It was said there was a stretch of swamp and muskeg so voracious seven sets of track were sunk, one on top of another, before the last finally stayed above ground. There was so much work blasting through the 500 million year old PreCambrian Laurentian Shield, a dynamite factory was built nearby to save transportation costs!

Prior to the three sisters, other ships served the expanding market for shipping immigrants west and hauling massive amounts of construction supplies for the CPR. The Owen Sound Transportation

NOVEMBER: THE CRUELEST MONTH

An ice covered Algoma *arriving in Port Arthur after a frigid November trip. Being part of the water - rail link for the CPR meant sailing in virtually any weather. Author Collection*

Company ran three ships between Georgian Bay and Port Arthur. The sidewheelers *Magnet* and *Sparton* and the propeller *Africa* were popular craft. The *Sparton* wrecked on Caribou Island but was later salvaged and the *Africa* was overwhelmed by a Lake Huron gale in 1895. The Collingwood-Lake Superior Line operated the propeller steamers *Compana* and *City Of Owen Sound* and sidewheeler *Francis Smith* to the north shore also.

1885 illustrated the extreme importance of a functioning trans-Canada railway for the security of the country. It was the year of the Riel Rebellion, aka Northwest Rebellion, Northwest Resistance or Saskatchewan Rebellion. Simply put, the Metis people in the Saskatchewan area under Louis Riel rebelled against the Dominion of Canada which they felt hadn't addressed their concerns for the survival of their people. Despite some early victories the rebels were ultimately defeated when the Dominion government was able to transfer troops from the east to the area of conflict. Most of the distance the Army covered by rail, but the section along the north shore of Lake Superior that wasn't finished meant they had to cover by marching. Since it was winter, they were forced to march on the frozen lake to the next railhead. Riel, of course, eventually danced the "Texas Two-Step" at the end of a rope, a fate not uncommon for rebels against the crown. And so ended the rebellion but it showed the critical importance of having reliable year around transit, something lake shipping couldn't provide.

The *Algoma* also had a brush with disaster early in her career. On May 25, 1885, downbound from Port Arthur, she stranded 3/4 mile west of the Two-Heart River Life-Saving Station in the eastern lake. The Life-Savers made eight trips out to the steamer in their surfboat but the seas stayed calm and she was released without damage, certainly a testament to her stout construction and very benign seas.

Louis Riel was a leader of the 1885 rebellion which illustrated the critical need for reliable trans-Canada transportation for national defense. Author Collection

Moving troops by foot over the vastness of Canada was not efficient thus railroad and shipping was vital. Author Collection

NOVEMBER: THE CRUELEST MONTH

She was almost empty on her final trip, carrying only five passengers in first class, six in steerage and a heavy load of 540 tons of cargo consisting of 200 tons of railroad steel, 100 tons of copper and 240 tons of general merchandise. In addition, there were 51-crew for a total of 62 souls on board.

At 4:00 p.m. November 5, she cast off from her Owen Sound wharf, her powerful engine wheezing steam and steadied on a course that would eventually bring her to the Soo. Foul weather was lashing the area which may have contributed to a lighter than normal passenger list. She locked through the Soo without incident the following day and reached Whitefish Bay about noon. There she raised her sails, stoked the boiler fires higher and raced along at 15 knots. The sails were used to help propel her if the wind blew fair and given her northeast tailwind, the time was right to use them. Port Arthur lay dead ahead and Captain John S. Moore intended to lose no time in completing his trip. After all, he had a schedule to keep! Moore was her original captain, bringing her over from Scotland the year prior.

Late on the night of November 6, Lake Superior spawned one of the ferocious fall gales for which she is infamous. The wind shrieked through the rigging and sails strained with the added pressure. Blowing snow obscured vision and combined with flying spray from the rising waves froze to the rigging and made the decks sheen like spun glass. The notorious November Witch came call'n.

By the morning of the 7th the gale had increased its tempo. Freezing rain was falling and the northeast wind piled the waves higher and higher. The *Algoma* still charged along like a ship possessed. Pushed by her engine and pulled by frozen sails she pranced through the seas with wild abandon. To continue on in such condition was insanity!

Captain John Moore ordered the frozen sails taken down. Struggling with stiff lines on an icy deck swept by freezing seas, his crew managed to get the job done but only because he ordered the wheelsman to swing a couple of points south to ease the strain on the canvas. Once the work was finished the wheelsman started to bring her back on the original northwesterly heading.

Moore knew he was dangerously close to the rocky coast of Isle Royale. His normal course probably would have carried him past the island's rocky north tip and a quick swing to port would bring him past Passage Island and into Thunder Bay and Port Arthur. His problem at the moment was compounded by uncertainty regarding his position. With near zero visibility and a strong northeast wind on his quarter, he could have been slowly pushed well south of his intended track and directly into the deadly reefs of Isle Royale.

Believing discretion the better part of valor, Moore decided to turn to starboard and the safety of the open lake rather than attempt to navigate the treacherous island coast without being certain of his position. Shortly after 4:00 a.m., the *Algoma's* bow began to swing northward toward the open lake and safety. Most of the passengers and crew were tucked away in their bunks, weathering the gale the easy way.

With a deadly shudder the *Algoma's* swinging stern ran hard up on one of the island's many underwater sentinels. Huge seas began sweeping over the impaled steamer in quick order. Flooding was reported in the engine room and after holds. The forward half of the steamer still floated free, rising to meet each wave, placing a terrible strain on the hull. To avoid a possible explosion when the cold lake water hit the hot boilers, Captain Moore ordered the engineer to blow off the steam, adding its steady shriek to the howling of the demented wind.

One of the young waiters remembered the horror of the wreck. "The captain told us there was great danger and the best place was down on the lower decks. We started to run there when the waves carried away the hurricane deck and we grasped the rigging. The captain passed a lifeline along and we hung on to it for over eight hours, believing that every minute would be our last. It was dark and freezing cold with a terrible sea. There were two ladies and three little girls that I noticed. They were swept away with the cabins, before which we could hear the ladies and girls calling piteously for help but no one could help them."

William R. McCarter, a passenger from Meaford, Ontario, with saltwater sailing experience claimed, "The waves rushed in great mountains over the decks and every few minutes the despairing shriek of some unfortunate persons was heard as they were carried out to sea and lost. The vessel lay broadside to the island and there was a dreadful surf - an awful sea pounding and beating against her sides. The cabin soon gave way and the women, children and men were

The stern stripped by the pounding sea. Author Collection

then washed off the boat beyond all hopes of safety... The electric lights went out a few minutes after the boat struck and the confusion and excitement were terrible... The captain alone remained cool and steady... I was standing between the captain and another man when the cabin came crashing down on the captain and pinned him to the ground... The man on the other side received a severe blow on his head and cried out, "I'm crushed, I'm gone!" The next great wave carried him off without the slightest struggle and he went to his death without a groan."

Mate Hastings later recalled going into the cabins to roust any passengers out and found a lady and her daughter crying uncontrollably in the saloon. Both were only wearing thin nightdresses, little protection against the piercing cold. While he was escorting them to a safer location and holding on the woman's hand, a wave burst through the saloon, sweeping the woman and daughter out into the lake! Eventually the mate led others to apparent safety in the rigging but in the fury of the storm the masts were later blown into the lake.

ALGOMA - A DAY OF GLORY, A DAY OF LOSS

The predawn darkness was broken only by the faint white flashes of waves breaking over the doomed ship. Moore huddled many of the survivors in the stern where he led them in prayer. A passenger remembered, "Before we rolled the captain up he said, "Men, let us unite in prayer," and with death staring us in the face we knelt down and the captain prayed for us all... During the night we could hear the captain inquire from the spot where he lay, a prisoner of his injuries, "How's the wind, mate?" and he seemed glad when he was told it was veering around to the shore side."

Lifeboats were knocked into splinters, woodwork snapped and hatch covers blown off by the pounding waves. Huge seas hammered the *Algoma* with pile driver force, slowly grinding her to pieces. The sounds of the storm were only pierced by the screams of passengers or crew swept overboard by the grasping water.

At approximately 6:00 a.m. a horrible tearing of metal rose above the howling gale. The bow ripped free just forward of the engine room and slipped beneath the waves, carrying with it many of the crew and passengers thought trapped inside.

As black night finally gave grudging way to gray dawn, the survivors still clinging to the stern saw they were separated from the island by a bare 70 feet of water! Although not apparent at the time they were over 8 1/2 miles south of the north tip of Isle Royale and perhaps a dozen miles off their intended course. It was a horrible miscalculation!

With courage born from desperation several crewmen attempted to reach shore in the last lifeboat, so far spared by the waves. Although the lifeboat capsized, some of the men did reach the rocky beach. Other's didn't. The overturned lifeboat and bodies were added to the cauldron of boiling wreckage. Masts, spars, lines and timber beams all floated together - tender morsels in Davy Jones's wicked stew!

The crewmen who made it to shore could do nothing to assist those trapped aboard the *Algoma*. All through the day of the 7th the storm raged although slowly decreasing in ferocity and eventually dying during the night. The following day those ashore made contact with the only inhabitants of Isle Royale, a group of fishermen. The fishermen rendered what aid they could sheltering the few survivors, including Captain Moore, in their small shacks. A makeshift raft built by the survivors on the *Algoma* reached shore after some anxious moments. Although Moore lived through the wreck, no one ever cast negative aspirations for surviving when so many others perished. Enough tales of his heroism circulated to negate any such thoughts. Warmed by bonfires the cold and hungry survivors waited for aid. It finally arrived on Monday the 9th when the *Athabasca* arrived. She was flagged down by an island fish tug as she was working through the Passage Island channel. Imagine the stunned disbelief of her captain when the crew of the tug relayed the horrible news of the wreck! Boats from the *Athabasca* soon rescued the 14 survivors of Lake Superior's greatest maritime disaster in terms of lives lost. It is interesting to note the *Algoma's* other sister, the *Alberta*, outbound from Port Arthur passed seaward of the *Algoma* at approximately the time she struck the reef, the blinding snow and gale preventing the *Alberta* from witnessing her sister's death. Captain Andrews on the *Alberta* was keeping watch for the *Algoma* since they usually passed near Passage Island. He later said the storm was so fierce, while he was making steam for 14 knots, his speed was a bare 3 knots! The waves had generally been pushing the *Algoma* but he was bucking head into them.

It is easy to say so many passengers and crew were lost with a given shipwreck. But when names and stories are attached to the dead, it is much more poignant. For example, Mrs. Dudgeon of Owen Sound was drowned with her six-year-old son and four year old daughter. Her husband in Winnipeg got a simple ten-word telegram saying, "*Algoma* gone down. Your wife and two children are drowned." The family of E. L. Frost, his wife and son were gone; so were the two young Buchanan brothers. Mrs. Shannon, the only stewardess on the ship, first and second engineers George Pettigrew and Alexander McDermott of Sarnia, Purser Alexander McKenzie and newsboy George Thompson, all lost. Many, of course, like the Dudgeon tragedy, destroyed families. Others had no loved ones and their deaths went unmourned. They simply ceased to exist and no one cared, just nameless victims of shipwreck.

Just two days after the survivors reached Port Arthur, Mate Hastings was back at the wreck in the chartered tug *Siskowit* searching for bodies and cargo. He was soon joined by the tug *Hattie Vinton* chartered by Mr. Dudgeon of ten-word telegram infamy. He immediately came from Winnipeg to search for his family. Only two

The Algoma *wreck represented the greatest loss of life of any Lake Superior shipwreck. Author Collection*

bodies were immediately recovered from the wreck, a wheelsman and deckhand. Both were discovered under huge heaps of wreckage ashore.[6] The searchers found no other remains and very little cargo: a couple of barrels of whisky, some cases of tea and a few sacks of nuts. The *Siskowit* swept the area around the wreck site and as far as Rock Harbor a couple of miles to the northeast. A week later the chief clerk of the CPR was at the site in the tug *Butcher's Bay* and found a couple of passenger's trunks and several bags of mail. More passenger relatives searched in the tug *Mary Ann* but all came up empty handed. The lake had swallowed the dead - forever.

A Canadian government investigation found Captain Moore guilty of being far off course and suspended his license for nine months. Although he sailed again as a master, he never again held steady command. The First Mate Joseph Hasting, on duty when she hit the reef, had his license suspended for six months. The investigators officially stated the cause of the disaster was, "...the ship overrunning her estimated distance and the failure of the officers to use the log as they should have done." The "log" is a "patent log," a mechanical device measuring the distance a ship traveled. In effect a rotator is pulled through the water astern of the ship, which registers the distance traveled on a dial onboard. While generally accurate, it is subject to freezing in very cold conditions. It is worth noting the only other navigation instruments available were the magnetic compass and a chronometer (clock). Navigating was certainly more art than science in 1885.

A measure of fault for the wreck was also placed on Henry Beatty, the manager of the shipping line. Some members of the public, both U.S. and Canadian, believed it was his pushing his captains to persistently keep to the schedule regardless of the weather that caused the disaster. Beatty came over to the CPR from the North West Transportation Company in 1882. His brother James continued to run the North West Company. The two lines were in strong competition. It was a case of driving on regardless of conditions lest the competition beat us!

The *Algoma* hit the southeast side of Mott Island, two miles northeast of the old Rock Harbor Lighthouse at a point often called Greenstone Rock. In the spring and summer of 1886, Captain F. I. Merriman and his hard hat salvage divers recovered the boilers, main engine and 13 smaller engines from the stern which had been swept

Wreckers worked on the Algoma *for several seasons. Rutherford B. Hayes Library*

The Manitoba *underway. Author Collection*

off its rock perch by winter storms. The divers also recovered 200 tons of miscellaneous scrap.

The 1886 salvage operation resulted in the addition of another name to Lake Superior's long list. The tug *George Hand* was blown up in shoal water by a sudden squall and wrecked. The crew was unhurt and her machinery later salvaged. She had already recovered the engine and off loaded it to the island when she had her accident. The next year the Port Huron tug *Challenge* was back at the site and recovered additional machinery and cargo.

The salvaged machinery was used in the new CPR steamer *Manitoba* built in 1889 by the Polson Iron Works in Owen Sound to replace the *Algoma*. Until she was ready, the CPR chartered the steamer *Campana*. The *Manitoba* continued in operation until 1950 finally being scrapped in 1951, all the while running on the *Algoma's* old engine!

In 1903 another salvage firm, using the small steamer *J.C. Suit*, attempted to recover the 250 tons of pig iron ballast as well as some of the steel and copper cargo. It was reportedly unsuccessful. Another salvage effort was made in 1905. Exactly how much was hauled up is open to speculation. Some books specializing in "treasure"

The beach opposite the wreck. Author Collection

shipwrecks still list her as containing her full cargo and even add $16,000 in specie as a "sweetner."

The *Algoma* was officially listed as a loss of $225,000 for the vessel and $17,000 for the cargo.

In August 1886, some very disturbing stories filtered out from Isle Royale. The tales charged some of the local fishermen rifled the bodies of *Algoma* victims and sunk the remains in the deep offshore water.

The stories evidently came from the wreckers working on the wreck. The divers reported only finding two bodies, both pinned in the framework of the steamer. Personal articles of value were discovered in the fishermen's cabins but whether they were taken from the bodies or simply washed up on the rocky shore isn't known. Captain Baker and the U.S. Revenue Cutter *Andy Johnson* visited the island and made inquiries concerning the affair but evidently couldn't find the truth for certain but there were those pesky stories. One claimed the fishermen disposed of the bodies by rolling them up in an old gill net, weighing it with some rocks and dropping the whole thing far off shore where no one would ever find them.

Considering searchers from Port Arthur were on the site within two days of the wreck, the fishermen had to act fast. While this is a limiting factor, it doesn't prevent their action. And since the wreck was very close to shore, the bodies should have come up sooner rather than later. If there were any to be found it would have been immediately afterward, before the Port Arthur searchers arrived. Incidents of folks ashore stripping the dead of valuables were fairly common on the Lakes, as well as saltwater, too. That it happened to the *Algoma* victims shouldn't be viewed as too unusual.

One of the legends of the *Algoma* involves her bow. Remember when the stern went up on the reef the forward half of the ship floated free, the violent motion of the storm eventually resulting in it breaking free and sinking her with many of the victims. Reputedly the bow has never been found, drifting off into deep water and plummeting into the icy depths. According to island folklore several commercial fishermen knew where it was since they soon fouled nets on something that wasn't there before the wreck. When they finally freed their nets the twine was streaked with rust. Thereafter fishermen stayed clear of the obstruction. Several sport diving groups have made efforts to find it but without reported success.

While the loss of life suffered in the *Algoma* wreck was horrendous, the worst of any Lake Superior shipwreck, consider the

The foredeck of the steamer Pontiac *was impaled on the bow of the* Athabasca *after a collision in the St. Marys River. Author Collection*

truly terrible disaster if she had carried a full load of passengers! She could have had more than 1,200 people aboard. If the same ratio of loss held, roughly 77% (48 of 62), 924 people would have perished! Consider too, she didn't carry enough lifeboats or life jackets for anything approaching a full passenger load. It would have been a freshwater *Titanic* 27 years early.[7]

The *Alberta* had her own involvement with shipwreck and death. On July 27, 1884, she cut down the wooden freighter *John M. Osborn* in a thick fog six miles northwest of Whitefish Point. Four of the *Osborn's* crewmen were lost in the disaster and one man from the *Alberta* trying to rescue one of those killed. In order to keep her schedule, the *Alberta* was running full speed regardless of the visibility.

The *Athabasca* didn't survive her career without a scrape or two. In July 1891, her captain got into an argument with the captain of the steamer *Pontiac* about who had how much of the channel in the St. Marys River. The result was a collision sinking the *Pontiac* and leaving a good part of her bow deck impaled on the *Athabasca*.

References:

Algoma File, Stonehouse Collection.

Annual Report, U.S. Life-Saving Service - 1886, 427.

Dana Ashdown, *Railway Steamships of Ontario* (Erin, Ontario: Boston Mills Press, 1988), 23, 55, 237, 239, 244, 246.

Ashland Press (Ashland, Wisconsin). November 14, 1885.

James P. Barry, *Ships of the Great Lakes* (Berkley, California: Howell-North Books, 1970), pp 25-29.

Mark Bourrie, *Ninety Fathoms Down, Canadian Stories of the Great Lakes* (Toronto: Hounslow Press, 1995), 101-112.

Dana Thomas Bowen, *Shipwrecks of the Lakes* (Cleveland: Freshwater Press, 1971), . 122-123.

Russell W. Brown, "Ships at Port Arthur and Fort William," *Inland Seas*, October 1945.

Captain Edward Carus, "100 Years of Disasters on the Great Lakes," unpublished manuscript, 1931.

Cleveland Plain Dealer. August 8, 1889.

Correspondence from the Canadian Pacific Railway, August 10, 1973.

Correspondence from the National Maritime Museum, Greenwich, England, August 31, 1976.

Daily Northwestern (Oshkosh). November 10, 1885.

Daily Times-Journal (Fort William, Ontario). September 22, 1933.

Dominion of Canada, Department of Marine, "Casualties to Vessels Resulting in Total Loss on the Great Lakes - From 1870 to Date," 1975.

Duluth Tribune, November 13, 1885, May 11, 1903, June 2, 1905.

Mac Frimodig, *Shipwrecks Off Keweenaw* (Copper Harbor, Michigan: Fort Wilkins Natural History Association, nd).

Skip Gilliam, "Memories of the Lakes," *Telescope*, March-April 1979, 31-36.

Harold A. Innis, *A History of the Canadian Pacific Railway* (Toronto: University of Toronto, 1971), 134-136.

Keith Krueger, "Last Voyage of the *Algoma*," Anchor News, January-February 1982, pp. 5-11.

Fred Landon, "Engines Salvaged From Lake Depths Powered the MANITOA," *Inland Seas*, Winter 1970, 313-314.

Ditto - *Lake Huron* (New York: Bobbs-Merrill Company, 1944), 313-314.

Ditto - "Sixty Years of the C.P.R. Great Lakes Fleet," *Inland Seas*. January 1945, 3-7.

"Marine Protest, Dominion of Canada, Province of Ontario, District of Thunder Bay, John Malcolm Munro, Notary Public, by John S. Moore, Master," November 9, 1885.

NOVEMBER: THE CRUELEST MONTH

John Mills, *Canadian Coastal and Inland Steam Vessels, 1809-1930* (Providence, Rhode Island: Steamship Historical Society of America, 1979).

Mining Journal (Marquette, Michigan), November 10, 11, 14, 1885, April 24, May 24, July 10, August 7, 14, 21, 28, September 13, 1886, July 23, August 27, 1887.

George Musk, *Canadian Pacific; The Story of a Famous Shipping Line* (Toronto: Hold., Reinhardt and Winston, 1981), 104-109.

"Notes," *Inland Seas*, January 1946, 56.

"Notes," *The Detroit Marine Historian*, October 1947, 7.

"Notes," *The Detroit Marine Historian*, November 1947, 10.

JOHN M. OSBORN, <http://www.boatnerd.com/>

Owen Sound Advertiser, April 24, 1884.

Portage Lake Mining Gazette (Houghton, Michigan), November 12, 26, 1885, February 4, 1886.

"Register of Wreck Reports, U.S. Life-Saving Service - 1885".

Harry E. Rieseberg, *Fell's Complete Guide to Buried Treasure, Land and Sea* (New York: Frederick Fell, 1972).

Walpole Roland, *Algoma West, It's Mines, Scenery and Industrial Resources* (Toronto: Warwick and Sons, 1887), 14-18.

Runge Collection, Milwaukee Public Library.

Reverend Peter van der Linden, ed. *Great Lakes Ships We Remember* (Cleveland: Freshwater Press, 1979).

Scanner, Monthly News Bulletin of the Toronto Marine Historical Society, "A Famous Trio Comes to the Lakes." January 1976.

ditto, "Ship of the Month No. 37 *Algoma*, *Alberta* and *Athabasca*." February 1974.

Shipping Times. <http://www.clydesite.co.uk/clydebuilt/viewship.asp?id=12713>

Toronto Evening Telegraph, November 5, 1932.

Bob Welnets, *Ships of the Great Lakes on Post Cards, Volume II* (Manitowoc, Wisconsin: Manitowoc Marine Museum, 1977).

W.R. Williams, "Shipwrecks at Isle Royale," *Inland Seas*, Winter 1956, 253.

Julius F. Wolff, Jr. "Canadian Shipwrecks on Lake Superior," Inland Seas, Spring 1976.

Ronald Wrigley, *Shipwrecked, Vessels That Met Tragedy on Northern Lake Superior* (Colbalt, Ontario: Highway Book Shop, 1985), 3-14.

Footnotes:

[1] There was an unforeseen consequence to the new CPR line. At the time Victoria, B.C. was the center of the North Pacific fur seal trade. With the railroad running straight through to the Atlantic, sealers could now consign their skins direct to the main London fur market. Much of the fur seal harvesting was centered in the Bering Sea, which the U.S. closed to foreign vessels claiming it acquired the rights to the area when it purchased Alaska from the Russians. Britain objected strenuously to the U.S. action. Since the trade was of great economic importance, it was possible things could get out of hand, leading to armed conflict. The whole mess was finally sorted out (kind of) by treaty in 1893. Had the CPR line not been completed when it was, the volatility of the situation would have been much less.

[2] Different sources give different numbers lost. The best estimate is 45-48. Since the purser with all the records was lost the true number will always be in doubt.

[3] The *Athabasca* was launched as the *Athabaska*. The name was changed before delivery to Canada.

[4] The rated passenger capacity is listed differently in varying sources. When she arrived in Canada one paper reported it as 180 first class and 1,200 steerage. Another claimed a total of 1,000 people.

[5] A camel is a buoyant device chained to the side of a ship to raise her and reduce draft or provide stability.

[6] There is some evidence two more were recovered within a couple of days and several others eventually showed up in fishermen's nets over the next couple of months. Establishing the truth of this is very difficult but it is not unlikely.

[7] R.M.S. *Titanic* sank on April 14, 1912 with the loss of 1,517 people.

MAUMEE VALLEY, BELLE SHERIDAN AND HENRY FOLGER - FOR WANT OF A LIFE-SAVING CREW

The death of the crew of the schooner *Maumee Valley* is typical of the dangers of sailing the Lakes late in the year, especially when the wreck occurs in a area without competent life-saving coverage.

The 214-gross ton, 127-foot, three masted schooner *Maumee Valley* was built in Maumee, Ohio, by F. E. Bugbee in 1868. She was in all ways a very typical sailing vessel of the post-Civil War era. Her wire standing rigging was a vast improvement over the old tarred manila. Capacity ran to 14,000 bushels and construction cost was estimated at $20,000. A Buffalo newspaper simply described her as "a craft of the size as floats on the lakes."

Her end came on November 22, 1900, when she was driven on the Point Pelee Middle Ground, Lake Erie, by a gale. She was carrying a full cargo of coal. Middle Ground Shoal is just southeast of Point Pelee Passage Light, about 5 miles southwest of Point Pelee. It is a very dangerous location for shipping. The entrance to the Detroit River is about 30 miles to the west.

Her seven person crew, six men and a female cook, tied themselves off in the rigging to avoid being swept away by the boarding seas but when help never came, they all froze to death in the ratlines. She was commanded and owned by Henry Scanlan.

The Canadian tug *Home Rule* attempted to reach them but was unable to do so. Considering the gale and shoal water this failure

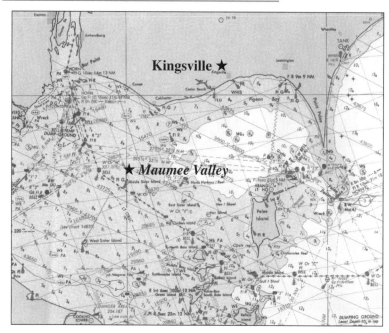

was understandable. The tug captain claimed had the lifeboat at Kingsville been useable they might have lived. Kingsville was 16 miles distant from the wreck, an inordinate distance for a lifeboat to travel under its own power, however, in similar circumstance American lifeboats were towed by tugs to the vicinity of the wreck, performing the rescue and returning to the tug. What precisely made the Kingsville boat "unusable" isn't known but it can be surmised it was a lack of general maintenance and repair. Without professional crews the everyday but critical things often weren't accomplished, the result being dead sailors.

The efficiency of the Canadian Life-Saving had always been problematic in comparison to the U.S. Life-Saving Service. While the latter was professionally managed and funded and operated by highly competent leadership and crews, the former was far more casual and reflective of a very inefficient attitude to the mission.

A good example of the state of even the few lifeboat crews employed was commented on in the Oswego Palladium of November 22, 1886: "The Canadian government employs no life savers, but those who man the boats have sixteen drill days during the year, receiving $1.50 each per day. Vessel men long since appealed to the

Canadian government to establish stations at points along the lakes and maintain paid crews but the government seems to have given the matter little if any attention." (Authors comment - drilling a mere 16 days a year is a joke when compared to the daily drill of the US crews throughout the entire navigation season!) Canadian volunteer stations were eventually established at Coburg (1882), Toronto (1883), Wellington (1883), Popular Point (1883), Port Rowan (1883), Collingwood (1885), Goderich (1886), Port Stanley (1885), Pelee Islands (unknown) and Port Hope (1889). Keepers were paid a paltry $75 a year, certainly not enough to consistently attract competent men. Originally the stations were given Dobbins lifeboats, which were very good indeed and were well liked by their crews. But it always comes down to the quality, training and courage of the men. It was a standard volunteer crews rarely met, U.S. or Canadian.

For a time in the 1840s - early 1870s on the Atlantic coast and 1850s - early 1870s on the Great Lakes, the U.S. tried to get by with providing only lifeboats to selected areas in the expectation volunteer crews would man them in time of need. In most instances it was a dismal failure. Finally, in the 1870s, complete and fully equipped and manned Life-Saving Service stations began to be established and made operational with stellar results. Additional stations were later added as resources allowed.

A Canadian life-saving crew was finally placed at Wellington the year after the *Maumee Valley* disaster. Wellington is about eight miles northwest of Salmon Point and whether the life-saving crew would have been able to reach the wreck is at best problematic given their lack of general proficiency. But if the station had been operated during the *Maumee Valley* wreck perhaps the outcome would have been different. The crew of the schooner may of lived.

The *Maumee Valley* got into her fair share of bumps and scrapes throughout her 32-year career. On May 12, 1898 she collided with the schooner *Vineland* in the Maumee River damaging her rigging. In 1880 she went aground on a shoal near Brockville in the St. Lawrence River. She was hauled off without damage after being lightered of 5,000 bushels of wheat. June 1874, saw her aground in the St. Marys River.

Earlier, the *Maumee Valley* had an especially tough time of it on Lake Erie while enroute from Toledo to Buffalo with 15,000 bushels of wheat. She sprang a leak in rough weather and to avoid sinking, her captain put her on the beach of Rondeau, Ontario. Once the gale blew itself out he apparently managed to back off and lay a course for Pt. Pelee where he again put her down in shallow water, the leaking being more than his pumps could handle. After being pumped out with steam pumps at least one of which was presumably kept aboard, she was towed to Detroit. Reportedly she had 3,000 bushels of wet grain, soggy evidence of his leaking hull. After reaching Toledo she was given proper repair.

In a flash of the disaster yet to come, in May 1883, she was ashore at Pt. Pelee but recovered without trouble. Her last accident was at Port Colborne, Ontario, on November 8, 1900. Heavily laden with barley and bound from Toledo to Buffalo she stranded early in the morning on a reef east of the harbor. She was on a rocky bottom, running out two feet forward. Three tugs tried to drag her free but were unable to do so until later that night. Her value was placed at a mere $4,000 and she carried no insurance.

The schooner W.R. Taylor *was similar to the* Belle Sheridan. *Author Collection*

The death of a crew through the lack of competent life-saving effort was not unique to the *Maumee Valley*. There were many other examples. The schooner *Belle Sheridan* left Charlotte on the American side of Lake Ontario at 8:00 a.m. Saturday, November 6, 1880, bound for Toronto with coal. Opposite Thirty Mile Point she was slammed by a southwest gale. The crew at once lowered the foresail and mainsail and headed their vessel on an east by north course. About an hour afterwards the blasting wind sent the mainboom over the side carrying away the yawl boat. At 3:00 a.m. the sea was running level with the schooner's rail and the main topmast gave away, crashing off into the blackness. At day break the crew sighted Presque Isle bluff, but the *Sheridan* was unmanageable and they couldn't make good a course to reach Presque Isle harbor. In desperation Captain James McSherry, Sr. let go the anchor but after holding a short time it began to drag, and the schooner went broadside on the bar off Weller's Beach near Consecon in eastern Lake Ontario. She slewed around with her bow heading north just off the beach about two miles from Presque Isle harbor.

Huge waves dashed over her until 1:00 p.m. while the crew held on as best they could behind the yawl bitts and windlass. Every few minutes a deluge of frigid water swept over them, soaking all to the bone. Captain Mc Sherry, Sr., was so cold he had to be grabbed tight by his three sons: John, Thomas and James, who themselves were so benumbed as to have scarcely any use of their limbs. Edward McSherry and Samuel Boyd, who were holding on to each other, soon lost the use of their arms, and James McSherry Jr. went to the assistance of his brother. Shortly afterwards the old captain died, his body washing down the deck and off the lee side into the black lake. Young Edward cried out several times that he could stand the cold no longer before dying in his brother's arms

The wreck attracted a crowd to the beach and several brave fellows tried to reach her in a small boat. They made three tries, failing each time. Realizing the hopelessness of the situation, James McSherry, Jr. determined to strike out for himself. Crawling aft to the main rigging he leaped into the tumultuous water and after being swept around the bow was carried half way to shore by a single wave. Another wave carried him closer still, and he was finally hauled to safety aboard the boat trying to reach the broken ship. Shortly after James made shore at about 5:00 p.m., the mainmast gave way and fell directly across the schooner smashing into the place where the remainder of the crew were holding on, apparently killing them all.

Those lost were James McSherry, Sr. Captain; John Hamilton, mate; 21-year old John McSherry; 17-year old Thomas McSherry; 13-year old Edward McSherry, and Samuel Boyd, all of Toronto. John, Edward and James were all the old captain's sons.

John Hamilton's body was later picked up on the shore about half a mile below the wreck, with his skull smashed; in fact, the whole top of his head gone. Another sailor's heart and lungs were picked up on the sandy beach. The other bodies must have been lashed to the rigging and as newspapers said, "torn to atoms." Scarcely a vestige of the wreck was left on the bar, the beach strewn with the debris for miles.

Captain McSherry, Sr. left a wife and five children, two girls and three boys (besides the two lost with him). The tragic news of the wreck was delivered to McSherry's wife in Toronto by impersonal telegram. No family friend gently broke the news. The local newspaper described Mrs. McSherry's distress as indescribable. The family were long time Toronto residents and Captain McSherry was well regarded as an honest well-meaning seaman.

The sole survivor, James McSherry, Jr., was an experienced sailor going "to sea" at age 11 as cook in his father's schooner *Echo*. He stayed with the schooner for three long years, the last as mate. He then shipped out before the mast in the schooner *West Wind* for two years. After she was wrecked off Coburg in 1879 he joined up as a sailor with his father on the *Belle Sheridan*. Even after surviving the wreck he wasn't soured on sailing although he did take a year off before joining the steamer *Arlington* for two years. He eventually became her captain, then commanded a succession of steamboats.

The 265-ton, 123-foot, two-masted *Belle Sheridan* was an old vessel, built at Oswego in 1852 by a Mr. Miller. After a varied career she was brought to Toronto and lay for several years sunk in the slip at Sylvester's wharf. She was eventually purchased by a Mr. Lamb of Toronto for a beggar's price of between $900 and $1,000. Lamb left her on the bottom until Captain McSherry purchased her as is, in February 1880. After raising her he put her back into a semblance of sailing order including new decks, and mainmast and a new

James McSherry Jr. had a long career following the Belle Sheridan *shipwreck.*
Author Collection

centerboard box. According to his wife, the captain, "laid out all the money he had upon her." As an indicator of the economic pressure he was likely under, the old captain also claimed he planned to make two more trips before laying her up for the winter. He was truly gambling with the gales of November.

In the summer of 1880, she was rated B-1 in the Canadian Register. She was valued at $4,000 and insured for $2,600. Capacity was about 12,000 bushels.

McSherry undoubtedly purchased the *Belle Sheridan* to replace his old ship, the schooner *West Wind*. Just before the close of navigation in 1879 he misread the lights at Cobourg harbour during a gale and put the west wind on the beach becoming a total wreck. The captain needed a ship. Money was tight and the old *Sheridan* was available regardless of her decrepit condition. Since McSherry previously worked as a ship's carpenter it is likely he and his sons performed most of the rebuilding work themselves.

Over 100 people were on the beach watching the *Belle Sheridan* disaster unfold. The helpless sailors drown before their eyes but they weren't able to help. Many eyewitnesses knew had there only been a proper lifeboat with a trained crew, every man on the *Belle Sheridan* could have been saved. Had only the Canadian government taken the initiative to start a proper life-saving service instead of sticking their parsimonious heads in the sand! Instead the carnage of death went on and on.

The *Belle Sheridan* storm killed 24 sailors besides those lost on the schooner, overwhelming two schooners and one propeller.

Another six schooners were driven ashore and a half dozen suffered other storm damage.

Like most old wind wagons the *Belle Sheridan* had numerous brushes with disaster. Perhaps the strangest occurred in January 1858, when she was moored for the winter in Oswego, New York. A spot of unusually warm weather caused a rapid snow melt which was partially held up by an ice jam on the river. When the jam finally let loose the resulting torrent of water slammed into six moored schooners, including the *Belle Sheridan* plus a canal boat, tearing them from their lines and sending them bobbing on out of the harbor! Since the several moored tugs were also laid up for the winter with cold boilers, it took nearly a day before one could be quickly sent out to search for the errant vessels. But instead of waiting for the tugs, a couple of captains loaded up two yawls with men and took off in pursuit. The sailors chasing after them in the yawl boats had a tough time of it but were finally successful in getting at least several of the schooners back to Oswego. However, when the lake blew up a day later reportedly the *Wide Awake*, *Adkins* and *Virginia* ended up going to pieces against the Port Ontario shore.

Just two weeks later another tragedy occurred within hailing distance of the *Belle Sheridan*. And again, had there been a Canadian lifeboat and crew available there likely would have been no loss of life. On November 21 the schooner *Garibaldi* went ashore about 7:00 a.m. also on Weller's Beach. She was bound for Toronto with a cargo of coal when slammed on the bar by a terrific gale. Like the *Belle Sheridan*, she attempted to reach Presque Isle but was unable to make it. Instead she dropped her anchor but when her hawser broke, strong winds sent her for the beach.

Folks on shore saw the disaster in the making and several men managed to battle through the waves to her with a small boat and rescue three of the crew including the woman cook. But they couldn't take anymore people aboard so three men, the captain, mate and a sailor, were left aboard for the night to face the terrible cold. When the rescuers were able to fight their way back out in the morning, they discovered two of the men were badly frozen and the third literally frozen stiff. The two still living had to be chopped free from ice holding them to the shrouds where they had lashed themselves. All night long the waves froze on the decks making the rigging into iron bars. Mate Louis Stonehouse, decided to take his chances below deck in the cabin where they found him dead, frozen in ice with his hands reaching up as if to ward off a terrible and certain death![1] Mariners knew it was just another death chalked up to the parsimonious Canadian government failing to provide a lifeboat.

Another example of the carnage caused by November gales and death by the lack of availability of a suitable lifeboat and crew is the misfortune of the three-masted schooner *Henry Folger* on Thursday, November 30, 1882.

The *Henry Folger* cleared Cleveland on Thursday, November 23, with a cargo of 693 tons of coal, bound for Brockville, Ontario, on the St. Lawrence River. The coal was intended for the Grand Trunk Railway Company.

Caught in a terrific gale and snowstorm she struck hard on Salmon Point Reef (AKA "Wicked" Reef) Friday night just east of Wellington, Ontario. When first spotted from shore she was about three-quarters mile off the beach with her mizzenmast gone and stern apparently stove. The dim shapes of two sailors could be seen, one of whom was lashed to the boom.

A volunteer crew made several fruitless attempts to reach the ill-fated vessel in a fishing boat but the still howling gale and breakers were too fierce to overcome, especially in such an ill-found craft.

About 9:00 a.m. her mainmast tumbled overboard followed by the foremast; a few minutes later the *Folger* started to break up completely and disappeared in the crashing seas. The *Folger* was commanded by Captain James W. MacDonald of Clayton, New York, and had a crew of eight men, including his 15-year old son, all of whom were lost. All the crew hailed from Clayton, New York. Reportedly the eight-man crew of another schooner was also aboard, pushing the death toll to 16. The second crew picked the wrong schooner to deadhead home on!

Marine men from Clayton who visited the wreck site reported nothing left of the vessel but the anchors and chains. One captain said he never saw such a complete wreck. The bodies of Captain McDonald and first-mate Watson Wiley were recovered and returned to Clayton for burial. The mate left a wife, and the captain, a wife and three children. It is worth noting Captain McDonald was a Mason

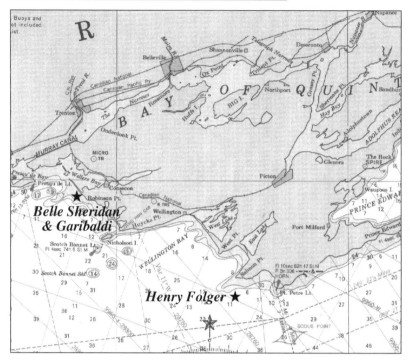

partially explaining the extraordinary efforts to recover his remains. He was also buried in Clayton with Masonic honors.

Bodies that came ashore were badly mangled by being beaten on the rocks by the surf making identification near impossible. They were quickly coffined and buried Saturday morning. There was no reason to delay. Large quantities of coal also washed ashore, certainly a boom to the folks along the coast. Many a home was heated that winter courtesy of the *Folger*.

The *Folger* had a rough go of it the week prior to her loss putting into Cleveland with her sails all split, having been out in a gale and obliged to run down past Port Colborne as she could not make that port.

The 133-foot, 326-ton schooner was built at Clayton, N.Y., in 1873, valued at $15,000 and insured for $10,000. She was owned by Folger Brothers of Cape Vincent, New York. Technically she was a "canal schooner," a sailing ship specifically built to navigate the –confines of the Welland Canal.

Traditionally two types of schooners were used on the Great Lakes; the "canaler" and the "upper lakes" schooners. The former was built with the size, hull and rigging to allow her to travel through the Welland and St. Lawrence River canals. From its first opening in 1829 until enlargement in 1846, vessels were constricted to 100 feet long, including bowsprit and mizzen booms, 22 feet in width and 6 in draft. After canal enlargement vessel size ratcheted up to 150 feet in length, 26 feet in beam and 9 feet in depth.

The effect of the restrictions was to force shipbuilders to built craft with stubby bows and very flat sterns necessary to "cram" the ship into the locks while still carrying the maximum cargo. In addition bowsprits and jibbooms were rigged to fold inward. Since bottoms had to be as flat as possible instead of the more traditional and effective "V" shape, retractable box centerboards were used. When entering a lock or canal the centerboard could be cranked up into the "box" inside the hold by the crew. Back on open water it would be lowered thus providing the theoretical "bite" needed to avoid slipping leeward in a wind. Retractable centerboards were also used on upper lakes schooners since they provided the same advantage entering shallow rivers and harbors.

In general, canal schooners were less strongly built than their upper lakes sisters and more prone to shipwreck and storm damage.

Considering the long tradition of the Royal National Lifeboat Institute in England, the utter and complete inability of the Canadian government to develop an efficient and timely comparable service is remarkable. Unfortunately, many good men and women paid for the official neglect with their lives.

References:

Buffalo Commercial Advertiser, January 28, 1858; September 14, 1868; November 13, 1880; December 3, 1882; May 9, May 10, 1883.

Buffalo Morning Express, May 13, 1898.

Chicago Tribune, August 20, 1868.

Detroit Free Press, November 9, 1900.

J.W. Hall Great Lakes Marine Scrapbook, November 1880, 1882.

Kingston Whig-Standard, November 8, 9, 11, 1880.

Mansfield, J.B. *History of the Great Lakes, Volume 1*, (Chicago: J.H. Beers and Company, 1899), 377-385.

New York Times. November 28, 1900.

Oswego Palladium, February 9, 10, 11, 12, 14, 19, 1857; November 13, 1880

Port Huron Daily Times, November 27, 1900.

Port of Toronto Shipping Register, Record Group I2 A I Vol. 239 National Archives, Ottawa.

Report of the Chief Signal-Officer of the Army - 1879, Washington, D.C. Government Printing Office, 1880, 747.

Report of the Secretary of War, Volume 1, Washington, D.C. Government Printing Office, 1874.

Runge Collection, Wisconsin Marine Historical Collection.

Toronto Globe, November 9, 1880; October 30, 1897.

Footnotes:

[1] No relation to Author.

MATAAFA -
SO NEAR BUT YET SO FAR

Without a doubt the most spectacular shipwreck to occur in Duluth was that of the *Mataafa* on November 27, 1905. The wreck didn't happen in a vacuum, rather it was one of a series of disasters in what some sources claim was the greatest storm to ever hammer Lake Superior. This point is of course debatable, but the tremendous damage the storm inflicted on shipping isn't.

While the storm in November was devastating, the entire year was atrocious for shipping. Fog, poor navigation, collision, ill luck

The steamer Clemson *made port in a near sinking condition. Author Collection*

NOVEMBER: THE CRUELEST MONTH

The wood steamer Hesper *wrecked near Silver Bay on Minnesota's North Shore. Author Collection*

and gales caused all manner of problems for ships big and small, old and new.

It started off in May with the 250-foot wood steamer *Hesper* wrecking near Silver Bay. While the summer was relatively quiet, when the fall gales came early there was hell to pay. In September the nearly new 468-foot steamer *D.M. Clemson* limped into port in a near sinking condition from storm damage. Battling through a gale off Knife Island, the whaleback steamer *Samuel Mather* lost a watchman when a monster wave swept him away to his death in a gurgle of foam. The same storm threw the 372-foot steamer *Sevona* on Sand Island Shoal, destroying her, sinking the 338-foot schooner-barge *Pertoria* off Outer Island. Although all her crew abandoned her safely, half were drowned when their lifeboat tumbled coming ashore. The worst September loss was the 291-foot steamer *Iosco* and 242-foot schooner-barge *Olive Jeanette* off the Huron Islands with all hands. The destruction by fire of the wood steamer *V.H. Ketchum* at Parisienne Island only added to the destruction.

October roared in with the wooden schooner-barges *Nirvanna* and *Galatea* wrecking at Grand Marais, Michigan, and the *Alta* at Grand Island. Gale winds blew the steamer *Oregon* ashore at Marquette and the 366-foot whaleback steamer *Frank Rockefeller* on the rocks at Isle Royale.

The wooden steamer Oregon *was blown ashore in Marquette's Middle Island Bay. Author Collection*

November began with the 238-foot wooden steamer *Portage* aground at Grand Marais and on the 23rd, the 255-foot wooden steamer *Charlemagne Tower Jr.* came creeping into the Portage Canal after a very bad storm battering.

The big steel steamer Monkshaven *smashed into Angus Island, near Thunder Bay. Author Collection*

The steamer Crescent City *ended up hard on a North Shore beach.*
Author Collection

But November really went to hell on the 27th when a blizzard roared into Duluth and western Lake Superior. The snow started around 6:00 p.m. and soon the wind was blowing at 44 mph. By the next dawn, winds were screaming 70 mph. For over 12 hours the wind never dropped below 60 mph and peaked at 79 mph. The blizzard knocked out telephones and telegraphs, blocked rail lines and streets throughout the area. The storm also disabled or destroyed 18 ships, one disappearing with all hands!

The 249-foot Canadian canal steamer *Monkshaven* smashed into Angus Island at the entrance to Thunder Bay, a total loss. The canaler *Rosemount* was luckier only stranding in the storm. When the scow *George Herbert* shattered to pieces on Two Islands, Ontario, on the northern shore three men died. Both the wooden steamer *George Spencer* and schooner-barge *Amboy*, ashore near Tofte, added to the carnage.

The 406-foot Pittsburg Fleet steamer *Crescent City* ran for three hours against the storm seas with her anchors down and her 1,600 hp engine straining at full speed but was still blown backward 20 miles into the rocky shore along the Lakewood area seven miles northeast

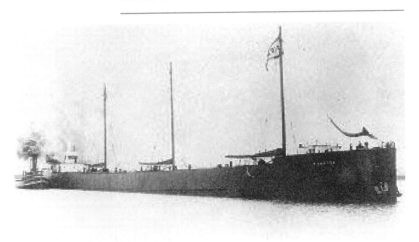

The barge Maderia, *another victim of the storm. Author Collection*

of Duluth. After breaking in two on the jagged rocks, she was so close to shore her crew pushed a ladder over the gap and scurried to safety.

The storm continued to pound the Pittsburg Fleet. Within an hour and a half and a mere 15 miles from the broken *Crescent City*, four more Pittsburg boats were wrecked. The 486-foot steamer *William Edenborn* was towing the 436-foot barge *Maderia* when the powerful storm tore into the pair. The *Edenborn* ended up cracked in two on the beach near Split Rock. Like the *Crescent City*, she was close enough to the beach the crew was able to cross on a ladder! Unfortunately, one man was lost when a boarding sea washed him into an open cargo hold. The *Maderia* went ashore on the rocks east of Split Rock breaking in two with all crew but one reached shore on a rope. The 454-foot steamer *Lafayette* and 436-foot barge *Manila* fared the same but on the north end of Encampment Island, northeast of Two Harbors. The barge crew quickly leaped to the nearby beach and used a rope to help the steamer's crew to shore. One man was killed when he lost his grip on the icy rope, plummeting to his death on the rocks below. The *Lafayette* was later demolished by the storm.

Split Rock today is famous for its very picturesque lighthouse. In fact the light was built in large measure in reaction to the terrible losses from the 1905 storms. The lighthouse was illuminated on August 10, 1910.[1]

NOVEMBER: THE CRUELEST MONTH

The salvaged stern of the Lafayette *entering the ship canal. K.E. Thro Collection*

The worst storm loss in terms of death was the 262-foot steel steamer *Ira H. Owen*, downbound from Duluth to Buffalo with grain under the command of Captain Joseph Milligan. Owned by the National Steamship Company and built in 1887 by the Globe Iron Works in Cleveland, she was one of the earliest steel steamers on the lakes. When the 380-foot steamer *Harold B. Nye* struggled into Two Harbors barely afloat Captain Alva Keller reported seeing the *Owen* in trouble about 40 miles off Outer Island in the Apostles during the height of the storm. She was blowing distress signals on her whistle

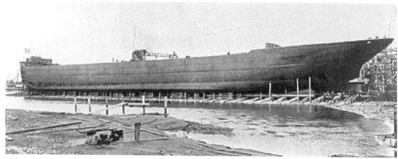

The Lafayette *was blown onto the shore at Encampment Island, near Two-Harbors. Author Collection*

Split Rock Light was largely built as the result of the carnage to shipping in the 1905 storm. Author Collection

but given the intensity of the storm and his own damages, he was helpless to assist her. He couldn't hear the actual signals but could see the tell tale puffs of steam shooting from her whistle. In the near hurricane force wind hearing anything was nearly impossible, sounds just blending together into a calliope of mind numbing noise. The *Owen* soon blotted out from view in a snow squall and when the snow cleared for a few minutes a couple of hours later, she was gone. When the Captain M. K. Chamberlain brought his *Sir William Siemens* into Ashland he reported passing through a large wreckage field a dozen miles east of Michigan Island. In it's midst were life jackets marked "*S.S. Ira H. Owen.*" She was gone with all hands.

While her loss in the storm can be simply explained as due to the storm, the fleet manager Captain J.J. Keith found it inexplicable. "I do not understand what could have happened to the *Owen*. She had a cargo of 116,000 bushels of barley, which was a light load for the ship. I spent three days in Duluth before the *Owen* sailed seeing that everything was in the best of condition. The hatch fastenings were all overhauled and made as strong as they could be. Why the steamer should had met disaster will always remain a mystery I fear."

Captain Keith's conclusion is still correct. She remains missing to this day, a victim of the storm that simply disappeared in its hungry maw. The best guess is her cargo shifted, a not unusual problem

The Ira Owen *was lost near the Apostles with all hands. Author Collection*

causing several vessel losses. Reportedly not a single body of her 19-man crew was ever found.

The Apostles saw the big 558-foot Pittsburg steamer *William E. Corey* driven up on Gull Island Reef. Point Abbaye, just east of the Keweenaw, became home to two more Pittsburg ships, the 413-foot steamer *Coralia* and barge *Maia*. The 416-foot *Western Star* was blown 125 miles south of her intended course to Thunder Bay and on to 14-Mile Point near Ontonagon. The 414-foot steamer *Brandsford* had a close call at Isle Royale. Bedeviled by the storm, she bumped onto to a reef off the east shore. Before the captain could even react to the disaster, a huge wave lifted her off the reef and back into deep water! Luckily she was light (without cargo), otherwise she would have remained on the rocky perch, perhaps forever. Only her constantly running pumps kept her afloat. She arrived in Superior in near sinking condition with many punctured hull plates and cracked frames. Her mate later commented, "In my 21 years of sailing on the Great Lakes I have never experienced such a storm."

Captain C. M. Ennes and the 416-foot steamer *Perry G. Walker* had a fearful experience. The two-year old ship left Duluth with a cargo of wheat bound for Buffalo about the same time as the *Mataafa*. Ten miles out from the canal she was overtaken by the blasting wind and blinding blizzard of the storm. Captain Ennes kept her on course until 8:30 p.m. when she was crippled by a series of truly monster seas. The waves smasheding her pilothouse and Texas windows, inundating everything and everyone inside with frigid water. The sledgehammer blows of the waves were so powerful they knocked the deckhouse four inches back from the bow! With little choice, Captain Ennes was able to skillfully turn the steamer around and run before the awesome seas. Without windows to shelter the pilothouse crew from the storm and spray they were constantly drenched with water, which soon froze giving the impression of ice men in an ice room. But the ice men were real, living breathing people, shaking near uncontrollably in the terrible cold. Ennes constantly rotated his watch below to give them a chance to warm up before facing the storm again, but it was brutal work! The *Walker* continued to run before the seas until reaching the North Shore where she tucked into Two Harbors for shelter.

When Captain A. Cummings brought his steamer *Isaac L. Elwood* in, she was in far more desperate condition. She hauled out of Duluth at 5:00 p.m. the day before, bound for Two Harbors to pick up the barge *Bryn Mawr* before heading for the Lake Erie mills. In the

The Bransford *"discovered" Isle Royale during the midst of the storm.*
Author Collection

blinding snow she couldn't find the Two Harbors Light and instead stood out into the lake to ride out the storm. She soon found out it was more storm than she could ride. Cresting waves regularly buried her forward half ripping off her hatch tarps and water flooding her hold. Displaying incredible courage, deckhands braved the open deck to secure the steel bars over the tarps several times to no avail. The waves continued to loosen them and the water in the hold grew deeper. At 8:00 a.m. Captain Cummings realized the situation was critical. He needed shelter and the best opportunity was Duluth. Timing the huge waves perfectly, he managed to turn the steamer and steady up on a heading for the canal.

After battling through the wild lake, the *Elwood* reached the canal shortly after 1:00 p.m. to find a maelstrom roaring at the entrance. Incoming seas smashed into the outgoing current to produce a boiling cauldron of seas. Ringing for full power, Captain Cummings charged ahead. A powerful wave smacked her starboard bow against the north pier, breaking several hull plates. The impact and a following wave pushed her stern into the south pier, battering more plates. But she continued on smashing her way through the canal and when she reached the inner harbor several tugs grabbed her, pulling her to shallow water off the Duluth Boat Club, where she settled to the bottom. It had been a close thing. Foundering in the canal would have been disastrous for lake shipping.

But the *Mataafa* wreck was something special. Not only in terms of loss of life, the desperate effort of the Life-Saving Service to save those crew they could, but also because the tragedy unfolding in front of the entire city.

The 429.6-foot steel steamer wasn't the biggest freighter on the lakes but was typical of the "long ships" hauling the rich Lake Superior iron ore to the flame and smoke belching steel mills of the lower lakes. For the folks in Duluth involved in the shipping industry she was a common visitor and in a sense represented "every ship."

The *Mataafa* hauled out of Duluth with her 365-foot consort barge *James Nasmyth* about 3:30 p.m., November 27. Both were loaded with Mesabi Range ore and bound for Lake Erie mills. Consort barges were common on the Great Lakes during this period. Moving bulk cargos is all about efficiency and towing a barge, wood or steel, behind a steamer proved highly efficient for the ore trade in particular.

Invariably the barges had small running crews aboard to take care of deck related tasks as handling lines or if need be, anchoring.

Once they cleared the Duluth Canal they encountered a fresh east-northeast wind and an air temperature bouncing on zero. The lake, however, was nearly flat with only a slight roll. Four hours later they were off Two-Harbors, 15 odd miles further up the Minnesota North Shore. The wind was now blowing gale force and thick snow was falling. Captain Richard. F. Humble on the *Mataafa* was following the traditional fall north course to the Soo, intending to run in the lee of the Canadian shore rather than taking the direct route along the south shore of Lake Superior. Only 32 years old, Captain Humble was from Conneaut, Ohio, and the lake was his life. He been a captain for six years and had the *Mataafa* since 1904.

By 2:00 a.m. on the 28th, the gale increased to a storm and both vessels were having a tough go of it. The violent seas were forcing the steamer off course and into the wave trough. Only with difficulty was she able to climb out of the hole dragging the barge behind. Huge waves were also rolling down her spar deck and smashing into the deckhouses as they were on the following *Nasmyth*. Realizing continuing on was foolish, Captain Humble swung back for Duluth running generally west-southwest. He later commented, "I have been sailing the lake 16 years; 6 years as captain, and I can truthfully say that this was the worst storm I ever encountered. The blizzard out on the lake was something terrible. The waves were the biggest I have ever seen them and were sweeping over the decks from both sides."

Captain Humble passed strict orders to his crew not to go on deck or leave the cabins. The seas were constantly sweeping the deck and the death was stalking the storm. Later he also related, "Even before we reached the entrance (author's note - Duluth ship canal) the force of the waves was so great that the steel bars on the fore and aft hatches were bent nearly double." The watchman remembered the waves "... were tossing the *Mataafa* around like she was a birch bark canoe."

Around 8:00 a.m. the wheelhouse crew heard the Two Harbors fog whistle blasting through the snow but the coast was invisible in the white blanket. Captain Humble could see only a few yards. He reportedly considered trying to make Two Harbors but with the blinding snow and difficulty controlling the steamer and barge in the storm he thought returning to Duluth was his best option. Remember,

The Mataafa *swinging wildly in the storm. K.E. Thro Collection*

this was prior radar, depth finders and even radio direction finding. Navigation was all by "dead reckoning," running a given course for a given time at a given number of shaft rpms (translating into speed/distance which could also be measured with a taffrail log). All the while, of course, taking into account variations for local compass deviation, wind, current and wave action. It was truly more art than science. Nevertheless, captains became extremely skillful at it, some extraordinarily so. Doubtless Captain Humble felt confident he could manage his way back to Duluth.

Because of the difficulty of precisely finding the piers in the blizzard he turned hard up into the seas several miles off. He wanted to gain some more sea room so when the weather lifted he would be in a better position to safely enter the harbor. He spent about an hour trying to get in the correct position all the while being battered by the huge combers rolling in from the northeast. Finally the snow cleared enough that he could confirm his position but he knew it was far too dangerous to try to bring the barge through the narrow canal with him. About two miles out he signaled Captain Graham on the *Nasmyth* to drop her hooks and ride out the storm. The *Mataafa* continued on alone for the canal.

MATAAFA - SO NEAR BUT YET SO FAR

The steamer must have been a real "sight" heading for canal. Monster waves smashing into her sending heavy deluges of water high over her decks, each threatening to overwhelm her as she gamely continued on, plowing through for the narrow entrance.

As she struggled closer the captain ordered her helm over to make the final turn into the canal. Deep in her engine room the machinery strained to give her all the power it had. About 2:15 p.m., just as she was approaching the canal entrance, a gigantic wave rolled under her stern and lifted it skyward which forced her bow down toward the bottom of the lake! Captain Humble later explaining, "we all felt her strike." The pilothouse was literally forced underwater, those in it holding on for dear life. The sudden action threw her off course and she crashed into the north pier striking with her starboard bow. Captain Humble tried to straighten her out with hard left helm but the stern continued to swing to starboard and the tremendous current running against the ship pushed her across the piers.

At this point there was a loud thud, the engine suddenly whined loudly and the black gang knew the prop had spun off. Without a screw she was utterly at the mercy of the storm. The same wave reportedly wrenched her rudder free, dropping it into the depths, the chief engineer exclaiming, "It's all up boys!" The current slammed into the dying steamer, slewing her around until she lay headed out into the lake and roughly parallel to the piers. Her portside yawl and liferaft and starboard boat were smashed by the seas and swept away. Driven by wind and wave the cold hulk of the steamer was drifting quickly for the beach. Both anchors were dropped but couldn't stop her, just bouncing along the bottom. She finally stranded off the north pier, port side to shore and stern about 500 feet out.

The crew was where you would expect them to be, doing the work expected of them based on their job. A dozen were aft, mostly the engine room gang, including chief engineer Claude Farringer and the remaining 15 men forward.

The men caught aft were in deep trouble; the freezing seas attacking them regardless of where they were trying to shelter. Massive waves hammered down the starboard gangway doors abreast the engine room and drove the men out on deck to find cover in the lee of the stack and deck ventilators. Since the boiler fire was the only source of heat, loosing it to the grasping lake was disastrous. Had the

NOVEMBER: THE CRUELEST MONTH

The Mataafa *striking the west pier. K.E. Thro Collection*

gangway door remained fast, it would have made all the difference in the world!

There was precious little protection. Breaking waves doused the men, the water freezing into deadly ice nearly as fast as it struck them. If they stayed where they were it was only a matter of time, and a very short time it would be, before they were dead from the penetrating cold. Their only hope was to reach the forward deckhouse. It was higher out of the water and less open to the hammering seas. To reach the comparative safety of the bow though, they would have to run hundreds of feet over the icy and wave swept deck. There was really no choice. Do it or die.

The second mate was the first to try to reach the bow. After supervising dropping the towline to the barge he remained astern waiting for the *Mataafa* to reach calmer waters rather than risk the open deck returning forward. Holding for a lull in the sweeping seas he nimbly ran over the deck and .....made it, arriving just after a wave boarded the open spar deck. Three more men waited for the right moment and dashed out on the deck. Two made it but the third, one of the firemen, was a couple steps too slow and was washed over the

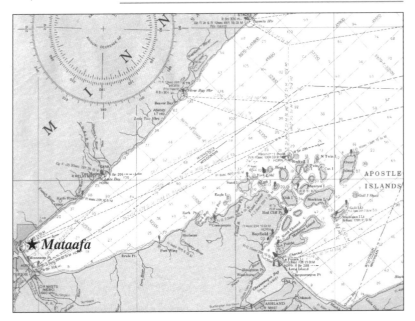

side by a wave. Incredibly he managed to climb back on board and kept going forward only to be swept over twice more. After the third time he gave up. Instead of trying again to reach the bow, he returned to the stern and curled up by the elevators.

One of the distinctions between the men on the bow and those on the stern may have been leadership. Under the direction of the ships officers, the men forward gathered all the blankets they could and burned the available oil lantern for added heat. The officers also kept the men moving to avoid freezing to death. But when the lamps burned out before dawn the captain was sure the end was near. He later related, "As a last hope I waded down along the passageway through three or four feet of icy water to the windlass room where I secured some kerosene, rags and dry matches, and by chopping down a bathroom door, I got some wood with which to build a fire. Then I went back. When I started the fire I called all hands down. We stood around the flames choking on the swirling smoke…"

One of the crew was more descriptive. "The waves pounded at the cabin. We danced about all night to the tune of that horribly gurgling water. It swept about our feet and shot through the doors and windows as though someone was throwing barrels of water at us. When we

The steamer Mataafa *being battered apart just offshore. K.E. Thro Collection*

were thirsty, we picked an icicle from the window and ate it. The icicles formed as quickly as we picked them."

The men remaining aft refused to try to reach safety in the bow. They apparently decided to take their chances on rescue rather than risk their lives going forward. In the breach, leadership aft was lacking.

About an hour and a half after the *Mataafa* struck, there was a sound like a cannon firing! The continuous pounding of the waves broke her in two about amidships. She later broke again between the original fracture and the bow.

There was some effort apparently made to get a line to shore. One man was seen by those ashore to throw what looked like a door into the water with rope attached only to have it quickly swallowed by the lake. Later a board came ashore in the waves with the message, "send Life-Savers in a hurry" scrawled on it.

The *Mataafa*, of course, wasn't the only wreck in that monstrous storm. Other ships narrowly escaped disaster. When the 330-foot steamer *Mariposa* came booming past the wrecked *Mataafa* and through the canal, crowds cheered. The word was out she was wrecked on the south shore so it was as if she rose from the dead, a ship given up for lost returning to port! That her stern cabin was smashed to pieces, and she was sheathed in ice a foot thick in places, only added to the drama of her unexpected ghostly appearance from the grave.

For the men on the *Mataafa*, especially those on the stern, hope faded quickly. Perhaps they were betting on the Life-Savers from Duluth Station. If they were, it was drawing to an inside straight.

Duluth Life-Saving Service Station circa 1910. The crew is "hitched-up" to the beach cart. Author Collection

The wreck drew a large crowd of spectators to the beach to watch the drama unfolding before their eyes. The crowd wasn't only on the beach exposed to the howling Artic-like winds and biting snow but also watching as the visibility allowed from many buildings. For example, an estimated 150 people were on the roof and sun deck of the Spalding Hotel. The rumor the captain had his wife and child aboard with him added more drama to the desperate scene.

Clearly the men on the steamer were in terrible peril but where was the Life-Saving crew? Why weren't they on the scene? Of course the impatient throng knew nothing of what was happening elsewhere along the storm wracked shore.

The Life-Saving crew was already enroute to a shipwreck but it was the 363-foot *R.W. England* stranded on Minnesota Point. The upbound *England* punched into the worst of the storm off Keweenaw Point and her only option was to keep driving on for Duluth. But she lost her course in the blinding snow and bumped ashore at 12:40 p.m., 2 1/2 miles to the southeast of the station. Luckily she was on an easy sand bottom and damage was minimal.

The Life-Savers received word of the wreck at 1:10 p.m. Keeper Murdoch H. McLennan quickly assembled his crew and they headed for the wreck with their beach apparatus cart. McLennan took over

The old Duluth Life-Saving Service boathouse. Author Collection

the keeper's duties in Duluth in September 1898. In his words as recorded in the station journal, "...there being a terrific sea running the street and road being almost impassable the sea going over the point...in some places we had considerable difficulty transporting the apparatus to the scene but finally arrived at 2:30 p.m. We found the steamship *R.W. England* bound from Ashtabula, Ohio, to Duluth light stranded about 300-feet from the beach with the sea going clear over her. We fired a shotline across the steamer about 2:45 p.m. which was instantly hauled aboard with the whip the hawser following as soon as the whip was made fast the whole being done very fast and without a hitch."

"The captain was the first ashore and informed keeper that he wished to telegraph his owners and requested that every man be taken ashore if they wished to leave the ship. The tenth man when taken ashore stated he was the rest did not wish to come until the captain returned. This was about 3:30 p.m. About 3:45 p.m. a man informed the keeper the steamer *Mataafa* of the Pittsburg Steamship Co. was ashore north of the north pier about a mile north of the station and was going to pieces. There being no immediate danger of the *England* going to pieces she being on a sandy bottom, keeper and crew instantly started back to the *Mataafa* over three miles distant."

The *England's* captain later related to reporters, "It was a wild night. It was impossible owing to the blinding snow to see anything and with the gale following us it was a night to be remembered. The seas came over the after house of the *England* and that will give you an idea of the way they piled up. It was one of the worst storms I have ever experienced." In a way he considered himself fortunate to have gone ashore where he did rather than face the horrendous conditions of running the canal.

He also provided a colorful observation of just how powerful the storm was and the desperate conditions on the boats. "About 9:30 this morning we sighted a steamer that looked like the *Mariposa*. She was loaded and the point that we sighted her was about eight miles below Two Harbors. She was pitching hard, and seemed to be in some distress. To give you an idea of how she was pitching, I could at times see 100 feet of her keel back from the forefoot, when she lifted on a big sea!"

Keeper McLennan continued his report: "Leaving all the apparatus except the haversack, lanterns and no. 1 and no. 4 shotlines which were brought back to the station on a hand sled, the gale, sleet and cold making the way extremely difficult. We arrived back at the station at about 4:20 p.m. and instantly started with the other cart and apparatus a crowd of about 100 people being at the station. The crew with the apparatus was quickly taken to the Government dock near the canal and loaded on a tug and taken to the lakeshore opposite the wreck, which was in a terrible condition being broke in two, her stern half constantly swept over by the terrific sea, her forward half being in a little bit better condition."

"The only place the apparatus could be worked with any chance of success was a narrow space between two houses and was covered with sharp rocks and boulders but the worst was the dense crowd jammed in the narrow space and was the cause of much valuable time being lost even before the apparatus could be unloaded."

Giant bonfires roaring on the beach provided both light and heat to those people huddling around the unfolding tragedy. The beacons also provided a small degree of hope to the sailors marooned on the dead steamer. A reporter was moved to comment the, "bright fire played upon the faces of pale men and sobbing women, all straining eyes toward the dark object on the horizon."

The keeper continued his report: "It was just dark when the first shot was fired, a no. 7 line. There being no signal from the wreck repeated signals from shore to haul away it was decided to haul the line back which broke near the ship. The next shotline fired was a no. 9 with the same result. This time it was decided to carry the gun to a point of rocks a little nearer but to windward of where the first two were fired. A no. 7 shotline was fired which fell over the pilothouse. As soon as the signal was seen (author's note - that the sailors aboard the wreck had the line in hand) that the shotline was aboard the shore end was carried back to the cart and whip attached. As soon as the signal was seen the whip was fast the hawser was bent on but in spite of every effort the two sides of the whip could not be kept apart owing to the narrow space and undertow and it fouled in the rocks out of reach and after a long time was finally cleared but almost at the same time both sides of the whip were cut on the bottom or by some wreckage near the wreck."

Captain Humble of the *Mataafa* later commented; "the shotline and trail line (author's note - actually the whipline) were tangled and frozen together. After fruitless efforts to untie them I cut the shotline. The mate went aloft, intending to tie the line to the spar. He couldn't do it however and I told him to fasten it to the shroud. This he did. When he came down he was so cold he could scarcely walk. His hands and feet were numb. Try as we could we couldn't get the breeches buoy to working."

Continuing the Life-Saver's report, "The whip was immediately hauled ashore and spliced into another tailblock. When it was decided to move the apparatus to the point of rocks from which the last shotline was fired. After everything was ready a no. 9 shotline was fired but could get no signal from the wreck. After repeated signals from the shore to haul away, the line was hauled taut and appeared to lead directly to the foremast and was seen next morning to be across the wreck about 50-feet after of the foremast. It was known that some of the crew were in the after part of the wreck but one of the company's men who was shouting through a megaphone claimed that he understood the captain perfectly shout back that they had all made

The broken Mataafa. *K.E. Thro Collection*

their way forward and were safe, three of them having made their way forward in the afternoon."

"It being clear there was no possible chance of launching a boat on the rocky beach in the dark it was reluctantly decided to cease operations till daylight. (author's note - Captain Watterson, shipping agent for the Pittsburg Fleet who was on the beach with the Life-Savers, recommended to the keeper to wait for morning before trying again. The Life-Savers were clearly exhausted and shaking with cold in their frozen oilskins.) The weather being bitterly cold and all the lines being frozen stiff could not be used to advantage after tying the shore end of the last shotline fired to a pole we left the scene about 11:30 p.m. determined to reach the wreck in some manner at whatever cost as soon as daylight appeared."

"We arrived for the boat at 1:00 a.m. the crew being greatly exhausted from being up during all of the night during the terrible storm and knowing the serious work ahead at daylight were given were given a rest till 4:00 a.m. About 4:20 a.m. we started back with Beebe-McLellen surfboat and rowed to Lake Ave. slip and got her hauled across the land to the lakeshore opposite the wreck. (author's note - the scene was positively eerie with the beach frozen into a sheen of ice and heavy frost mist hanging thick over the water and the white surfboat being pulled through the gray mist by oil skin clad surfmen.) The first launch was successfully accomplished at 7:30 a.m., the seas greatly diminished but still very high. After a severe struggle we got alongside. When we learned the terrible condition on the wreck the nine men aft all having perished being buried under the ice or washed overboard. We took seven of the survivors on board and started back and when near shore was caught by a wave that filled the boat but did not capsize and was nearly dashed against the rocks, landed safely. The last trip made successfully at 8:30 a.m. when eight were landed, fifteen in all. All the men were taken to a hotel (author's note - St. Louis Hotel) in cabs by the Co. We arrived back at the station at 12:00 p.m. At 3:00 p.m. the sea having greatly diminished, at request of company keeper being uptown with telegraphers No. 1 (author's note - Surfman No. 1 was the senior man in the absence of the keeper) went to wreck with surfboat and found four of the bodies under ice near the smokestack and delivered them to the company's man at Lake Ave. slip and returned to station at 7:00 p.m."

Keeper McLennan tended to understate the difficulty of the surfboat rescue. In spite of the early hour a large crowd was on the beach and they cheered loudly when the surfboat started out. No sooner had the men made several good strokes than a huge comber smashed into the boat, knocking the bow rower off his seat and flooding the boat with icy water. But the water streamed out the freeing ports in silver showers and she continued to battle out to wreck. The crowd gasped when the small boat dropped down the far side of a wave, answering with a welcoming sigh of relief when it reappeared.

Since waves were still washing over the steamer the Life-Savers had to be very careful how they approached. Carefully picking their chances they managed to dash in to the lee side several times, picking up seven sailors who slid down the near frozen rope and into the wildly heaving surfboat. In an act of true thoughtfulness, the Life-Savers passed up a lunch and some brandy to the men left aboard the steamer.

When the Life-Savers made shore with the first batch of survivors the crowd again broke into cheers. Spectators were so eager to get a close-up look at the victims they nearly mobbed them as they stepped from the boat.

Captain Humble later stated if she hadn't lost her lifeboats trying to enter the canal, he thought every member of the crew would have been saved. "The boats were the best lifeboats built and the raft was a good one, too." He also had thoughts about the men lost on the stern stating, "If the men in the back part of the boat had tried to come forward when we ran aground they would doubtlessly have been saved, but they waited too long before making the attempt." It all goes back to leadership.

Later the Life-Savers commented on the horror of the men frozen in the stern. Two of the sailors had "great gaping wounds" in their skulls giving the impression they were thrown headlong against some part of the ship, killing them violently. The chief engineer was grasping the base of the stack, perhaps striking his head on it or the deck. The steward was discovered forward of the stack, with his skull broken at the base and lying with this head in the hatchway, evidently tossed there by the boarding seas. His body was terribly contorted, legs twisted up behind his back. Both bodies were deeply encased in ice. The body of a fireman was found lying on his back with arms outstretched in the lee of the stack. It too was covered with ice. The most ghastly victim was a deckhand found in the ventilator on the lee

A lifeline can be seen running fore and aft over the weather deck in this remarkable photograph of a lake in storm conditions with boarding seas. Author Collection

NOVEMBER: THE CRUELEST MONTH

STEAMER "MATAAFA" WRECKED OFF PIER OF DULUTH SHIP CANAL, DURING THE GREAT STORM OF NOV. 28, 1905. NINE MEN WERE LOST FROM THIS VESSEL.

A cigar box cover celebrates the wreck. K.E. Thro Collection

side. A hand was clutching each side while his lifeless eyes looked shoreward for rescue that never came. The body, too, was implanted in ice.

All of the remains were so deeply enmeshed in ice axes were needed to free them. The chopping job took two very long hours to finish. The grotesque frozen shapes that once were living sailors made lowering them to the lifeboat and transport ashore all the more difficult. The spectators still lining the beach were doubtless shocked by their appearance. This was death, very up close and very personal!

The *Mataafa* was launched as the *Pennsylvania* at Lorain, Ohio, on February 25, 1899 by the Cleveland Shipbuilding Company for the Minnesota Steamship Company. After only a few runs she was renamed *Mataafa* to comply with a company policy that all ship names start with MA and end in A. When the Minnesota fleet was absorbed by the Pittsburg Steamship Company in 1901, the name remained.

Captain Tom Reid of Sarnia, Ontario, salvaged her the following year. Two years later she was back in Duluth and in deep trouble again, ramming and sinking the steamer *Sacramento* in Rice's Point Channel on October 14, 1908. Four years later she smashed into the steamer *G. Watson French* off Grosse Point on Lake St. Clair, receiving major damage. In 1946, she was converted to an automobile carrier for the Nicholson Transit Company and finally scrapped out in Hamburg, Germany, in 1965.

Some ultimate good did come from the *Mataafa* wreck. Federal steamship regulations were changed to require a safety line between the rear of the pilothouse and forward end of the aft cabin. Pulleys attached to the line with long ropes allowed the crew to, "make fast" and move fore and aft without danger of being swept off the open deck by boarding seas.

Captain Richard Humble continued his sailing carrier with the Pittsburg Fleet, the wreck of the *Mataafa* not being held against him. Apparently he left the lakes in 1916, dying three years later.

References:

Abstracts of Casualty Reports From the Life-Saving Service Annual Reports 1876-1914, NARA, RG26.

Annual Report, U.S. Life-Saving Service 1906. NARA, RG 26, pp. 97, 109, 142, 28-34, 238-241, 391.

Ashland Weekly News, September 6, 1905.

Captain Richard F. Humble - <http://archive.boatnerd.com/archivep/1-07/00006ebb.htm>

Captain Edward Carus, *100 Years of Disasters on the Great Lakes*. Unpublished Manuscript, 1931.

Daily Mining Journal, September 27, December 4, 1905.

Duluth Evening Herald, November 26 - December 2, 1905.

Duluth News-Tribune, May 1 - December 2, 1905.

Great Lakes Journal, March 1939.

Reverend Peter van der Linden, ed., *Great Lakes Ships We Remember, Volume III*, (Freshwater Press, Cleveland, 199), 212-214.

"Journal of the Life-Saving Station at Duluth, November 27 - December 2, 1905," NARA, RG 26.

NOVEMBER: THE CRUELEST MONTH

Lawrence A. Brough, *Autos on the Water, A History of the Great Lakes Automobile Carriers*. (Columbus, Ohio: Chatham Communications, 1987), 25-29, 37, 53-54.

Skip Gillam, "Marine Salvage, Your Best Market for Obsolete Ships," *Telescope*, September-October 1979, 129, 133.

Marine Review, August 23, 30, October 18, 1906.

Mataafa File, Stonehouse Collection.

Mining Gazette (Houghton, Michigan), November 30 - December 3, 1905.

"Postcards From the Edge," *Lake Superior Magazine*, December-January 1996, 72.

Donald Powers, "Shipwreck, the *Mataafa*: Agony on the Point," *Lake Superior Magazine*, October-November 1989, 73-77.

Footnotes:

[1] Split Rock Light is the most famous lighthouse in Minnesota. Of course it is also almost the only lighthouse in Minnesota.

JOHN OWEN
AND MYRON -
A DOUBLE LOSS

There must be something about the name *Owen*. Eight ships with *Owen* as part of the name perished on the Great Lakes. Two, the *Ira H. Owen* and *John Owen* were lost with all hands in Lake Superior. To date, neither has been found but remain among Lake's fleet of the missing.

The *John Owen* departed Duluth on November 11, 1919, bound for Midland, Ontario, with a cargo of 100,000 bushels of wheat. The 289-foot "composite" freighter was built in Wyandotte, Michigan, by the Detroit Dry Dock Company in 1889. Between 1878 and 1890, the company built nine such vessels. A composite ship was one with a hull built of iron framing with oak planking fastened longitudinally. Iron or steel plates covered the wood from the waterline to the main deck. At the time iron hulled vessels were not thought to be good risks by the insurance companies as compared with those built entirely of wood in spite of the fact iron ships were in use on the lakes since the *USS Michigan* in 1844! The ship was named for John Owen, a Canadian born Detroit businessman who was a principal in the Detroit Dry Dock Company.

When Captain George E. Benham of Lakewood, Ohio brought her out of the Duluth Canal it was into a rough lake, rolling seas, blowing northwest and fits of snow. But freighters don't make money by

NOVEMBER: THE CRUELEST MONTH

The John Owen *sailed off into a crack in Lake Superior never to be seen again. Author Collection*

laying in port when the weather turns foul so it was drop the dock lines and run the track for the Soo.

Below Devil's Island in the Apostles, the 440-foot *Edwin N. Ohl* passed her and later reported she appeared to be in good trim and running well. At the time the wind had shifted fresh southwest and snow squalls still bounced over the lake. When the *Panay* picked her up off Manitou Island at the tip of the Keweenaw, she also looked in good condition. About ten miles east of Stannard's Rock Light, the master of the upbound *Howard L. Shaw* passed her about 3:00 p.m. on the 12th. She still seemed to be in good order, running before the seas and not taking any aboard. Two hours later all hell broke loose. The wind cranked up to 60 mph accompanied by blinding snow and heavy seas. Some ships reported gusts of 70 or greater.

During the storm the big 580-foot Pittsburg Fleet *D.M. Clemson* briefly saw the *Owen* struggling with the storm. However, this is not the same as saying she was in trouble.

The fierce tempest drove shipping in to such shelter as they could find. Vessels in the St. Marys River either dropped their hooks or laid up to a convenient lock wall. Until the front blew through, there wasn't any sense in heading up Lake Superior.

When the *Owen* didn't lock through the Soo on schedule it was initially felt she was just sheltering somewhere. The 266-foot *Griffin*

When the OHL *saw the* Owen *she was proceeding without difficulty. Author Collection*

was missing, too. She was another old-timer built by the Cleveland Shipbuilding Company in 1891. Later she turned up safe at the Soo after riding out the worst of the storm in the protection of the Apostles. The 460-foot *M.A. Bradley* made it to the Soo a day late after sheltering at Isle Royale. Her captain said the storm was so powerful he kept rolling his rail under water! She also arrived at the locks with an estimated 100 tons of ice on her deck.

Finally a wireless message was sent out asking shipping to keep an eye out for the missing *Owen*. All reports were negative. Her location remained unknown.

It wasn't until the steamer *Westmount* passed through a wreckage field 20 miles south of Caribou Island the mystery of why the *Owen* didn't arrive at the Soo was at least partially answered. Caribou Island is about 60 miles northwest of Whitefish Point and roughly in the middle of the lake. The *Westmount's* radio call brought the Great Lakes Towing Company tugs *Iowa* and *Alabama* out to search but they found neither survivors nor the hull of the ship.

When the tugs stopped at Grand Marais, Michigan, their crews told Benjamin Truedell, the Coast Guard Officer-In-Charge of the Life-Boat Station, they found part of the pilothouse bobbing around off Caribou as well as significant wreckage including hatch cover shutters, table boards and her nameplate 10 miles southwest of the island. Truedell was the old Grand Marais Life-Saving Station keeper. When the Life-Saving Service combined with the Revenue Marine in 1915 to form the Coast Guard he stayed on, changing his title but not his job. Locally he was still called, "captain" but this was not his military rank.

From examining the floating wreckage the tug master thought the *Owen* sank slowly with waves washing over the top of the decks and

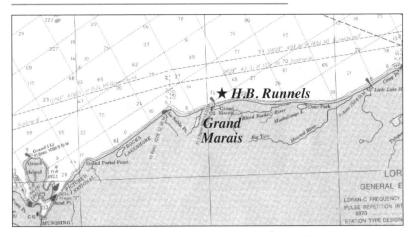

battering off parts of the cabin. Other pieces of timber were twisted, mute evidence of the great strains she endured.

Several fish tugs from Grand Marais also went out into the still rough lake to search for the *Owen*. However, the U.S. Coast Guard cutter *Cook* that happened to be visiting in the harbor stayed safe at anchor. Reportedly her captain said the lake was, "too rough" and he, "…would rather be on the ocean than lakes." Once the lake calmed, the *Cook* did search for floating bodies without success. The *Cook* was a 110-foot ex-Navy sub chaser and while seaworthy was ill-suited for work on the lakes. Twenty-two of the class were turned over to the Coast Guard from the Navy following World War I. A total of 440 were built for the Navy as wartime expedients and intended strictly for inshore patrolling. To save yard space for bigger ships the sub chasers were constructed by small yards throughout the country, including Great Lakes. Since some of the yards never built ships before, results were "spotty." With their wood hulls and triple gasoline engines, they were uneconomical and difficult to maintain. Most dropped off the Coast Guard rolls within several years although the *Cook* was retained until 1935 when she was surplused out but reacquired for World War II, finally decommissioning in 1945.

Few of the *Owen's* crew's remains were ever found. Running eastward, the big 545-foot steamer *Wilpen* passed through wreckage for ten miles from Manitou Island off the Keweenaw, running east, including an upside down lifeboat and a body in a life jacket. The captain reported it was too rough to pick up the body so it was left

The Coast Guard Cutter Cook *was fortuitously in Grand Marais harbor when the* Runnels *wrecked.* Author Collection

adrift. Days later, when the big 580-foot steamer *William P. Palmer* was locking through the Soo downbound the captain told a lock keeper they sighted another "floater" 40 miles west, northwest of Whitefish Point. Again, it was too rough to recover it.

The remains of the second engineer was located in a block of ice along the shore the following spring by the Crisp's Point Coast Guard Station crew and three more came up on Parisienne Island in Whitefish Bay. The body of the second engineer, William J. Reilly, eventually morphed into a famous "Life-Saver" ghost story of the Shipwreck Coast. Apparently his was the only body ever recovered from the area in spite of several earlier and erroneous news reports.

There was a crew of 22 aboard the *Owen* including one woman. Magnus Peterson and his wife were listed as the stewards. Also aboard were three officers, two wheelsmen, two watchmen, four deckhands, three engineers, three firemen and three coal passers. The breakdown by duty provides an interesting look at how a typical steamer of the period was organized.

Ten members of the crew were registered in the Lake Carrier's Association benefit plan enabling their beneficiaries to receive a death benefit of $207.50. The Lake Carriers also offered a reward of $25 for each body recovered and wired descriptions of the missing men to all the Coast Guard stations.

NOVEMBER: THE CRUELEST MONTH

The Wilpen *passed through* Owen *wreckage 10 miles from Keweenaw Point's Manitou Island. Rutherford B. Hayes Library*

Her metal lifeboat was discovered by a fisherman floating upside down on her air tanks off Maminese Harbor, north of Coppermine Point on the Canadian side of the lake. There were no oars or rudder. The boat was also freshly painted and deeply scratched, giving the fisherman the belief at one time she did carry *Owen* crewmen.

The lifeboat discovery sparked a tirade by some mariners against the use of metal lifeboats. One mariner complained, "The only reason for their use is this that they need little care during the season. Wooden lifeboats have to be put in the water once or twice monthly at least. The "tin pans" do not." A Coast Guard officer with North Atlantic convoy experience during the late war was quoted saying, "you never heard of us using them." He later elaborated, "I'll wager if the *Owen* and *Myron* (author's note - yet to be discussed) had been equipped with the sort of liferafts we use there would not have been a life lost, unless of exposure."[1]

The bias against metal lifeboats, of course, is so much illiterate claptrap. Metal lifeboats have been in service since the 1840s with great success. One version manufactured by John Francis was used by the U.S. Life-Saving Service, an organization with a stellar reputation for not tolerating poorly performing equipment.

JOHN OWEN AND MYRON - A DOUBLE LOSS

The 3,127 gross ton *Owen* was owned by the Owen Transit Company of Cleveland and a loss of $90,000.

As mentioned, the name *Owen* was not a lucky one on the lakes. The first *Owen* lost was the sidewheeler *John Owen* burned at Port Huron in April 1860. The two-masted scow-schooner *D.R. Owen* sank in a gale on November 1, 1878, while trying to enter the harbor at Manistee. Her history is a bit clouded as she was also reported lost with all hands on Lake Superior in December 1872, and wrecked near Ontonagon in September 1874. A scow-schooner is very different from a traditional Great Lakes schooner. Instead of having a deeper, curved bottom, theirs was flat. While it allowed more cargo and a shallower draft enhancing ability to navigate shallow rivers and harbors, it also decreased seaworthiness. Instead of a sharp stem and rounded stern, the scow-schooners had very blunt bows and square sterns. Describing one as a box with sails isn't far off the mark. Think of a scow-schooner as made by a farmer and a traditional schooner by a real shipbuilder and the difference becomes clearer. As the result of her less than seaworthy design and sometimes landlubber construction techniques, their use in open water was problematic. In short a scow-schooner was a shipwreck waiting to happen but they were cheap to build and thus disposable.

The 90-foot wooden propeller *Owen* went ashore on Gull Shoal near Long Point, Bay of Quinte in Lake Ontario on October 12, 1902, becoming a total loss although there was no loss of life. Reputedly, a broken steam pipe caused the disaster.

The 262-foot steel steamer *Ira H. Owen*, discussed earlier in this book, sank in Lake Superior with all 19 hands during the great storm on November 28, 1905. She was last sighted in distress near Outer Island, in the Apostles, and it is presumed she was lost there.

The 165-foot freighter *Monohansett*, launched as the *Ira H. Owen* in 1872 and renamed 10 years later, burned and sank off Thunder Bay Island, Lake Huron on November 23, 1907.

The 62-foot tug *Owen* was built in Detroit in 1881 and renamed *Marion E. Trotter* from 1908-1920. She regained her original moniker in 1921 and burned to a total loss in Port Huron on December 6, 1921.

The 196-foot schooner-barge *George B. Owen* wrecked twice, the first in Ashtabula, Ohio, in 1898. Thought a total loss her documents were surrendered but after reconsidering her condition shipbuilder

James Davidson rebuilt her, returning to service. On October 1, 1926, she swamped off Grosse Point in the Detroit River and sank. There was no loss of life.

And last but not least is the *John Owen* of 1919.

When the Grand Marais Coast Guard crew learned of the loss of the *Owen* they had just finished a rescue of incredible courage and daring. In fact it earned them the Treasury Department Gold Life-Saving Medal, the most prestigious recognition of non-wartime bravery awarded by the U.S. Government. Some of the surfmen were still recovering from injuries suffered in the rescue and there was little they could do but keep an eye open for wreckage and bodies. The story of the rescue illustrates both the violence of the storm that sank the *John Owen* but also the courage of the Grand Marais Coast Guard crew and the local volunteers that risked their lives so others may live.

On November 14, while the *Owen* was fighting her losing battle with the storm, the 178-foot steamer *H.B. Runnels* was upbound for the Keweenaw with coal when she sailed into the hell of wind and wave.

When dawn broke the lookout in the Grand Marais Coast Guard lookout tower saw the *Runnels* anchored about a mile off the station. She wasn't showing distress signals but the experienced surfman sensed she

The 178-foot Runnels *wrecked off Grand Marais. Rutherford B. Hayes Library*

JOHN OWEN AND MYRON - A DOUBLE LOSS

Benjamin Truedell was the legendary keeper of the Grand Marais Station but he was on leave and missed the Gold Medal rescue. Author Collection

soon would be, so he alerted Number One Surfman Alfred E. Kristofferson, in charge since Keeper Truedell was on leave. Benjamin Truedell was a legend along the Lake Superior shore. A veteran of many thrilling rescues, he picked a bad day to take leave. But it was the job of the Number One Surfman to step up when the Keeper was absent and Kristofferson was ready to do his duty.

He had the crew prepare the 36-foot motor lifeboat in case it was needed and had the lookout keep a close watch on the steamer. Kristofferson also went out to the *Cook* sheltering in the bay from the storm, and asked the captain for volunteers in the event rescue was needed. Several surfmen were ill or injured and with Truedell gone, he was effectively short another man. The captain agreed to help in anyway he could but pointed out he had a guest aboard that could really be of value, John O. Anderson, the veteran keeper of the Chicago Life-Saving Station. Anderson volunteered to help immediately. Kristofferson and his crew were absolute strangers to Anderson but every Service crew was trained to the identical standards so he was fully comfortable they knew their jobs and crew equally so with Anderson.

As Kristofferson and Anderson were walking back to the station they heard the mournful blasts of the steamer's whistle start blowing distress signals. It was time for action.

When the pair approached the boathouse they noticed the 36-foot motor lifeboat anchored off the dock. A surfman explained when they saw the distress signal they fired up the boat intending to pick Kristofferson up from the *Cook* but the engine stalled and they had to anchor and wade ashore.

With the power lifeboat out of the picture, Kristofferson went to Plan B. The station crew with volunteers from the *Cook* and Grand Marais Lightkeeper, dragged the surfboat and beach apparatus cart to the shore opposite the *Runnels*. The 26-foot oared *Beebe-Mclellan* surfboat was the second of the station's two boats.

Ex Life-Saving Service keeper Anderson, shown in the post 1915 photo holding a telescope, was critical during the Runnels *rescue. Author Collection*

Stranded broadside to the seas on a sandbar, the steamer was 500-600 yards offshore. Wave after wave smashed into her, sending spray high into the air and coating her in a thick layer of ice. Her crew of 17 men faced certain death as she slowly broke up in the hammering seas.

As second nature molded from years of drill, the surfmen set up the breeches buoy equipment including Lyle gun. After charging it with a maximum load of 6 ounces of Dupont's Life-Saving Powder, it was carefully aimed at the steamer and adjusted for offset from the wind. Normal maximum range for the Lyle gun was considered 400 yards. Even allowing for error in estimating the distance, it was a very long shot.

Waiting patiently until the wind lessened a bit, either Kristofferson or Anderson, pulled the lanyard and the small gun boomed, sending the 19-pound projectile out into the wild storm, a light shotline trailing along behind. The billowing line dropped neatly across the bow of the steamer.

Using the thin shotline, the *Runnels* crew quickly hauled the one-inch diameter whip line aboard, securing the block to the steering wheel post in the wheelhouse. With the block secure the men ashore could now haul away, pulling a heavy 2-inch diameter hawser out to the wreck. Once it was fast to the steamer, the shore end would be secured to a sand anchor and made taut as possible. When the breeches buoy, nothing more than a pair of heavy canvas short legged trousers sewed to a life ring was attached to the hawser with a snatch block, the crew ashore could haul men to safety one at a time with the whip line. In an hour or so all could be safe on the beach. Such rescues were commonplace in the old Service.

However, this time it all went wrong. Since the *Runnels* was laying parallel to the shore, a vicious current was set on the lee side. The long whip line was caught in the current, which spun the whip block as it was hauled out, fouling both ends of the rope, in effect twisting the rope around itself. Thus fouled, it couldn't be used to pull out the heavy hawser. Plan B failed so on to Plan C.

The surfmen brought both ends of the whipline together to form a double line and rove the surfboat painter (author's note - short line from the stem of a boat) over the doubled line making it fast to the bow. In effect they made a big loop around the doubled whipline. When the shore end was cinched up and made fast to the sand anchor, the surfboat now had a direct path to the wreck.

The surfmen climbed aboard the surfboat and took their places. On Anderson's command, the rest of the Coast Guardsmen from the *Cook* and local fishermen pushed the wagon as far into the surf as possible, dropped the front axle shoved hard on the stern and she shot off the rollers into the angry lake.

Even with the whipline's guide, getting out to the wreck was a hellish trip. Several times waves swept surfmen out of the boat, others quickly hauling them back inside. Spray froze on their faces and clothes. Hands made rigid with cold, grasped oars, and backs strained to keep the boat moving toward the steamer. Ice clogged oar locks and scuppers.

Their difficulty wasn't over when the surfboat finally reached the wreck. The waves on the protected lee side were running so steep she couldn't lay up to the wreck; instead, sailors slid down the whipline hand over hand and into the wildly surging boat.

The surfmen made four trips through the horrendous surf to save all 17 men on the *Runnels*. The last run was the most difficult. Instead of the 8 rowers normally used, only 6 men were still able to pull an oar. The others, including *Cook* crewmen, lighthouse keeper and several local fishermen, were exhausted or injured. There were only two sailors to take ashore on the last trip but they were the greatest challenge. The captain and engineer were both elderly, which meant a rope was fastened around each man as a safety measure when they slid down the whipline into the boat. Both men dropped off short, landing in the water, and had to be manhandled into the surfboat. Since the engineer weighed in at 315 pounds, it was backbreaking work to roll him over the gunwale. The *Runnels* broke up 30 minutes later.

Only three of the surfmen had the stamina to make all four trips; Kristofferson, Anderson and Russell Martin. Kristofferson was washed out of the boat twice and Anderson three times. True the old Life-Saving Service motto, "Regulations say we have to go out, but they say nothing about coming back," both men kept coming back for more, again and again.

The first trip out was a pure Coast Guard crew but as the men suffered from cramps from exertion and violent shaking from emersion in cold water, others took their places. Two of the volunteer fishermen were former members of the old Life-Saving crew and knew the drill well. A place in the surfboat wasn't for the fainthearted or lily-livered landlubbers. It was a man's job and Grand Marais had the men to do it!

As hard as it was for the men in the surfboat, it was equally hard though in a different way for their womenfolk waiting ashore. One witness stated there was no "...whimpering among the wives ...who stood on shore and waved encouragement..." Huddled together for mutual support they watched in apprehension for their husbands, sons and fathers. Those who waited also suffered, perhaps even more.

When survivors and rescuers made shore, frozen clothing and life-jackets had to be cut off. The men were physically done in.

It is worth noting the captain of the *Cook*, G.R. O'Connor, was the senior officer on the scene and therefore the man responsible for Coast Guard actions. There were (and certainly are today, too) officers who would take command, issue orders, take personal charge to, "make certain it was done right." The fact they didn't have a clue what they were doing never stopped a senior officer telling others what to do and in turn mucking up an otherwise well run and efficient operation. O'Connor, however, was a different breed. He knew Kristofferson and Anderson were the experts and he trusted them to do their job, reinforcing them with manpower from the *Cook* as they asked.

However, when he saw how exhausted both men were after bringing the last boat in to shore, he relieved Kristofferson from all station duties and ordered the clearly exhausted Coast Guardsman to

The lumber hooker Myron *was a victim of the same* Runnels *storm.*
Author Collection

bed. This was an extraordinary thing to do since regulations were clear in the absolute necessity to return all equipment to the station and prepare it for immediate use. He also relieved the crew from the night beach patrols and assigned one of the *Cook* crew to nurse injured surfman, Glen Wells. He had returned from the hospital after a serious operation just prior to the rescue but it didn't stop him from taking his place in the boat. He wouldn't let his buddies down. The old-time Life-Savers truly were iron men in wood boats! After the first desperate run through the breakers he had to be carried back to the station and the attention of a local physician. The same doctor was kept busy as other injured men reached the station.

When Keeper Truedell returned on the 16th, he went to work setting the station back in order to prepare for another call out. Still shorthanded with sick and injured surfmen, Truedell used local men to recover and maintain equipment.

It is interesting to consider what emotions must have churned in Trudell's mind when he returned and learned of the tremendous rescue. While his own courage and leadership were never questioned, he ably demonstrated both many times since the station opened in 1901, it still must have gnawed at him that he, "missed the big one." And yet there certainly was an element of pride that the men he trained performed so extraordinarily well in his absence.

The *Runnels* rescue demonstrated the indomitable spirit and courage of the old Life-Saving Service crews and the early Coast Guard. It was only four years since the old Life-Saving Service and Revenue Marine combined to form the new Coast Guard and the strong backbone of the Life-Savers was still much in evidence. For an organization essentially without organic history or tradition, the Life-Saving Service provided a powerful link to a heroic past.

In recognition of their bravery Gold Life-Saving Medals (Treasury) were awarded to each man who manned an oar, including Anderson and the volunteer Grand Marais fishermen.

Forty-five miles east of Grand Marais and a week later, another ship was fighting storm-striven Superior and like the *Owen* and *Runnels*, losing the fight. On November 22 the 186-foot lumber hooker *Myron* and her tow, the 194-foot schooner-barge *Miztec*, were downbound from Munising for Buffalo. The steamer carried 17 men under the command of Captain Walter Neal and the barge 7. As

The Myron *dropped the tow to the* Miztec *when things got "tough."*
Author Collection

typical for the trade, their holds were packed tight with lumber with heavy deck loads piled above.

When the pair left Munising's East Channel, the wind was blowing a light breeze from the southwest. Considering they were running in the shelter of the Pictured Rocks, the lake was likely almost flat calm. Such conditions were too good to last long and two hours out from Munising the wind hauled around northwest and cranked up to a severe gale. Instead of being sheltered by the shore, they were now being driven into it.

Mountainous waves slamming into their quarter and sending shards of water over the decks were sharp reminders of the power of the big lake. It is probable seams opened on both vessels as they worked in the seas and water ran fast into the holds. With heavy snow and plunging temperatures, thick ice formed, not only affecting the center of gravity but also the ability to rise to the seas. The *Myron* only had a 700 horsepower engine and strained heavily to keep moving toward Whitefish Point. Once around the point they could anchor and wait out the storm. However, the steamer was getting the worst of the ordeal and was slowly becoming sluggish as the water inexorably rose in her hold.

Help was in sight. About 2:40 p.m. Captain McRae on the 420-foot freighter *Adriatic*, also downbound, saw the pair were in trouble and ran his ship close inshore checking his speed to match their very

The 420-foot Adriatic *tried to rescue the* Myron *crew. Author Collection*

slow headway. He was using his bulk to provide a lee for them, sheltering both from the worst of the waves.

There are two versions of what happened next. Both are reasonable. The first goes something like this: Off Vermilion Point, about eight miles from Whitefish Point, Captain Neal made a difficult but necessary decision. For the *Myron* to have any chance of making Whitefish he had to drop the *Miztec* tow. He simply didn't have the power to make Whitefish Point with her dragging along behind. It wasn't a completely heartless choice. She would likely ride out the storm easier with her anchors down than straining at the end of towing hawser. Signaling his intention to the *Miztec*, the maneuver was completed and the *Myron* continued to fight on to Whitefish with the *Adriatic* providing vital escort.

The second version holds about 20 miles west of Whitefish Point the *Miztec's* rudder failed, which in turn over stressed the towing hawser, breaking it, and casting her to the mercy of the storm. She promptly dropped both anchors and safely rode out the storm. Later the steamer *Argus* picked her up and took her to shelter behind Whitefish Bay where the she waited until the tug *Iowa* brought her to the Soo. The *Myron*, dreadfully beset by the storm, continued on for the Point.

JOHN OWEN AND MYRON - A DOUBLE LOSS

Meanwhile the sharp-eyed lookout at the Vermilion Point Coast Guard Station watched the drama of the slowly sinking steamer and realized its significance. Sensing trouble coming, he alerted the keeper. Watching the unfolding situation through the eyes of long experience he made his decision. The small hooker wasn't going to make it so he manned his motor surfboat and headed out into the wild lake. Getting the boat through the surf and over the outer bar was difficult and very dangerous but it was their job and the Coast Guardsmen did it well. They knew if the hooker took a dive the best chance for the crew to live was if their boat was close at hand. The motor surfboat slammed through the waves trying to catch up with the *Myron*. It was an eight mile long chase.

About a mile and a half northwest of Whitefish Point, the *Myron's* boiler fires finally flooded out and without power she slipped into the trough. It was approximately 5:45 p.m. The crew quickly ran for the two small lifeboats and managed to get both safely into the water. Technically the boats were yawls; work boats rather than true seaworthy lifeboats. Within minutes the hooker sank, spewing out a tremendous field of floating wreckage including the deck load of lumber. The mass of lumber soon surrounded the lifeboats, trapping them within.

In the gathering darkness Captain McRae and the *Adriatic* twice tried to reach the survivors with his ship but the big steamer twice touched bottom. He could hear the men crying for help but the water

The lookout in the watch tower at Vermilion realized the danger the Myron *was in and sounded the alarm. Author Collection*

was too shallow for him to get any closer. All he could do was lay off and wait for them to come to him. When he was certain they were drifting too far inshore for him to help, he steamed around Whitefish Point and finding the steamer *Earling* anchored under it, asked her to radio news of the sinking to the Soo.

Another vessel was watching the deadly drama. Captain P. Francis Lawrence of the big 520-foot steamer *H.P. McIntosh* managed to force his way through the seething wreckage field close enough to the lifeboats to actually toss ropes to one. But the *Myron* crewmen were so numbed by the penetrating cold they couldn't grasp the lines with their frozen hands. The men in the lifeboats could only look up at the men in the big steamer with the pleading eyes of the living dead. Also fearing for his own ship bottoming out, Captain Lawrence was forced to back out into deeper water.

Meanwhile the Vermilion Coast Guard crew finally caught up with the wreck but the boiling mass of timber kept them from reaching the lifeboats either. Their wooden motor surfboat couldn't force it's way through the wreckage; so near to safety but yet so far.

The Coast Guard keeper knew the two *Myron* lifeboats would soon be destroyed by the wreckage around them and that the whole mess was rapidly drifting past Whitefish Point. If anyone survived the ordeal, and it was a very unlikely if, his best chance to find them was to get ahead of the wreckage and let any survivors come down to him. So he laid the helm over and went 20 miles deep into Whitefish Bay turning off Parisienne Island slowly working his way back. The night was black as sin but the Coast Guardsmen did their best. They found nothing and were forced to shelter at the Whitefish Point Light Station for the night.

The only survivor from the *Myron* was Captain Walter Neal who was in the pilothouse when she sank.[2] As the steamer settled, the pilothouse broke off and he climbed out through a window and onto the roof. He hung on for nearly a day until finally being picked up by the steamer *W.C. Franz* near Parisienne Island in Whitefish Bay. The *Franz* crew was on the lookout for bodies but surely didn't expect to find a living captain! Although he was still alive, Neal suffered greatly. His hands and fingers were so swollen from the cold, two finger rings were invisible, swallowed by the flesh. He also was unable to walk. In spite of his injuries, he eventually recovered to sail again.

JOHN OWEN AND MYRON - A DOUBLE LOSS

His jaws were nearly locked from the cold. When he was eventually able to talk he related, "had I not taken a large chaw of tobacco from the wheelsman before the ship sank it's probable that my jaws would have been paralyzed completely by the cold." He didn't spit it out until he was aboard the *Franz* 20 hours later, saying it kept his jaws moving and preventing them from freezing solid!

The story goes Neal was only saved because of an especially powerful set of glasses in the *Franz's* pilothouse. It seems W.C. Franz gave them to the steamer's Captain Jordan as a present and when the captain saw something unusual in the water four miles distant, the glasses enabled him to spot Neal's slowly waving arm.

Once safe aboard the steamer, Neal said he, "never felt anything so good as the heat in the *Franz's* cabin." He said he always enjoyed heat and at home he regularly kept the temperature at 90 degrees! The *Franz* continued on to its destination of Fort William with Neal and he remained aboard on the return to the Soo.

Anecdotal evidence suggests the bodies of all 16 remaining crewmen were recovered in the general vicinity of Salt Point, about 11 miles west of Point Iroquois. Fishermen found some bodies floating at the southern end of Whitefish Bay still wearing their lifejackets. The yawls the men were in when the *McIntosh* tried to reach them were battered to pieces in the heaving cauldron of timber and wreckage, leaving the dead crewmen to drift off into the black night in their lifejackets.

Other bodies were discovered frozen into ice along the shore, searchers literally having to chop them free. Another man was found wedged among the rocks in a reef off Salt Point. He was crammed in so tightly and so encased in ice he couldn't be removed until the lake was perfectly calm. Chisels, hammers and prybars were the tools of choice to free him.

Getting the remains to the Soo and the nearest funeral parlor wasn't easy. Some were taken to the train station at Strongs, Michigan, but it was a long and difficult trek of a dozen miles through the snow covered forest traveling on very primitive trails. Others were taken to the Soo by boat.

One man involved in recovering the remains described them as, "frozen and stiff in grotesque and gruesome forms." At the funeral home they were placed in front of a roaring fire all night just to thaw them out so they could be properly "laid out"! It must have been a scene directly out of H.P. Lovecraft's fertile imagination.

Local tugs scoured the bay and freighters were on alert, too. The Coast Guard Cutter *Cook*, with Captain Myron Blodgett the *Myron's* owner aboard, circled Parisienne Island and scoured the south shore of the lake. The loss of the *Myron* was a difficult experience for Blodgett. He told reporters all of the crewmen were personal friends and many were neighbors. Continued rough weather and snow squalls made it a demanding search. The big Canadian Pacific Railroad steamer *Alberta* also circled Parisienne Island looking for both survivors and bodies. Blodgett later offered $25 for each body recovered.

Some of the remains recovered after the initial flush of the wreck were eventually interred in the little Indian cemetery above Point Iroquois. The graves are still bordered by a small fence and marked simply, "Sailors of the Str. *Myron*." A local mill produced the rough coffins for them.

Flotsam from a shipwreck can add value to the local community. The keeper at Point Iroquois Light on Whitefish Bay discovered a chair floating in the waves. He waded out into the cold water to haul it to shore, discovering it not only was a "captain's chair" but also had *Myron* burned into the back. The chair proved a welcome addition to the sparsely furnished lighthouse.

Captain Neal was extremely upset over the failure of the *Adriatic* and *H.P. McIntosh* to rescue his crew. He charged criminal behavior against both captains.

His whining complaints eventually caused a special investigation by the U.S. Steamboat Inspection Service. During an open hearing Neal stated, "I was clinging to the roof of the pilothouse when the *McIntosh* hailed me shortly after the *Myron* went down from under me, not more than 16 feet away. Although it was dusk, the ship was so close that I had no difficulty in making out her name. I talked to the captain and expected he would put out a yawl and pick me up. He did not do so, nor any attempt in any way to help me. I will have a boat sent for you, the captain of the *McIntosh* called. And he drew away. I have never seen him since, nor do I ever want to see him by the great hokey pokey."

The Steamboat Inspectors from Marquette who conducted the investigation, agreed with Neal and the licenses of Captains Lawrence of the *McIntosh* and McRae of the *Adriatic* were revoked for, "failure to render assistance." The marine community was livid, feeling the penalty was totally uncalled for considering the effort both men made to rescue the *Myron's* crew. Unfortunately records are not available whether the verdict was appealed to higher authority and the outcome of that appeal.

While it is recognized Captain Neal as he was hanging on to the pilothouse roof, was in obvious distress, the ability of the two captains to assist him and his men was very limited. Both men took their ships into very dangerous waters in a desperate effort to reach the *Myron* crew. Captain McRae actually bumped bottom, something that could have sunk him immediately. Captain Lawrence managed to work close enough to get ropes to the men. That they couldn't handle them was beyond his control. As with the *Adriatic*, Lawrence, too, was in dire danger of striking bottom. Had either ship bottomed her stern, damaging the rudder or screw, the likelihood of wrecking on the lee shore was near certain. Putting a yawl down to rescue Neal was virtually impossible especially considering the horrendous conditions the Coast Guard surfboat was fighting through and it was a specially designed boat with a highly trained crew. The best Lawrence could do was a boat with a scratch crew of sailors with no training in managing a boat in such horrible conditions.

Neal claimed he was in 30 feet of water when the *Myron* sank, plenty of water for either vessel. What he failed to understand, or perhaps choose not to consider, was 30-feet is plenty of water when the lake is calm but in a powerful storm ships draw considerably more water as they roll and pitch, making them easy prey for a bottom strike. He also didn't consider the effect of large ships with underpowered engines, typical for steamers of the time, being forced into wave troughs and driven on lee shores.

While doubtlessly a bitter man with an axe to grind, the Steamboat Inspectors clearly over reacted to Neal's emotional and ill-reasoned complaints. After all, Neal managed to sink his own ship by coming out into conditions he should have taken care to avoid. It needs to be remembered that a captain's first and foremost responsibility is to the safety of his own ship and crew, and any risk taken must be carefully weighted. Both captains did that when they pulled their ships out of shoal water to safety.

NOVEMBER: THE CRUELEST MONTH

The *Myron* was fairly old for a wood steamer when lost, launched in 1888 at Grand Haven. Originally named the *Mark Hopkins* she was renamed *Myron* in 1902. She was owned by Captain Omar Blodgett of Duluth and named for Captain Myron Blodgett, the owner of the lost *Runnels*. With a single hold amidships, she had a capacity of 950 tons or 700,000 board feet of lumber. She was a loss of $45,000.

References:

Annual Report of the U.S. Coast Guard 1919, Government Printing Office: Washington, D.C., 1920.

Betty Byrnes Bacon, *Lighthouse Memories*. (Brimley, Michigan: Bay Mills-Brimley Historical Society, 1989), 13.

Bowen, Dana Thomas. *Shipwrecks of the Lakes*, (Cleveland: Freshwater Press, 1971),

Dwight Boyer, *Great Stories of the Great Lakes* (New York: Dodd, Mead and Company, 1966), pp. 264-269.

Donald L Canney,. *U.S. Coast Guard and Revenue Cutters, 1790-1935*, (Annapolis: Naval Institute Press, 1995), 79-81.

Correspondence, U.S. Steamboat Inspection Service, John *Owen*, NARA, RG 26.

Correspondence, O.M. Maxam, Chief, Division of Operations, U.S. Coast Guard to Prudential Insurance Company, October 19, 1920, NARA, RG 26.

"Daily Journal of the Coast Guard Station at Crisp's Point, November 20-29, 1919." NARA, RG 26.

"Daily Journal of the Coast Guard Station at Vermilion Point, November 20-29, 1919," NARA, RG 26.

Detroit Free Press, October 23, 1989.

Dispatch, U.S. Coast Guard from Cutter *Cook*, November 20, 1919, NARA, RG 26.

Duluth News Herald, November 14-18, 1919.

JOHN OWEN AND MYRON - A DOUBLE LOSS

Duluth News-Tribune, November 14-16, 1919.

Evening News (Sault Ste. Marie, Michigan), November 12, 14-15, 17-20, 24-29; December 2-9, 1919; March 24, 1920.

Marquette Mining Journal, November 14 - December 6, 1919.

Manistique Pioneer Tribune, February 27, 1964.

W. A. McDonald, "Composite Steamers, Built by the Detroit Dry Dock Company," Inland Seas, Summer 1959, 114-116.

Alexander C. Meakin, *Master of the Inland Seas, the Story of Captain Thomas Wilson and the Fleet That Bore His Name*. (Vermilion, Ohio: Great Lakes Historical Society, 1988), 100-102.

Owen (various), www. Boatnerd.com.

John Owen File, Stonehouse Collection.

"Report of Casualty, U.S. Coast Guard," *John Owen*, NARA, RG 26.

Runge Collection, Wisconsin Marine Historical Society.

Frederick Stonehouse, "The Gold Medal Shipwreck," *Wreck and Rescue Journal*, Volume 1, Number 1, U.S. Life-Saving Service Heritage Association, Spring 1996.

Telegram, Crisp's Point Station to Superintendent, 12th District, March 22, 1922, NARA, RG 26.

Telescope, May-June 1977, 73.

U.S. Steamboat Inspection Service, Report of Investigation, Loss of *John Owen*, January 6, 1920, NARA, RG 26.

Upbeat, "Shipwreck Victims Washed Ashore to Lonely Grave," February 4, 1970, 16-20.

William D. Wilkinson and Timothy R. Dring, *American Coastal Rescue Craft: A Design History of the Coastal Rescue Craft Used by the United States Life-Saving Service and the United States Coast Guard*. (Gainesville: University Press of Florida ,2009), 22, 33, 119.

NOVEMBER: THE CRUELEST MONTH

Richard J Wright, *Freshwater Whales, A History of the American Shipbuilding Company and its Predecessors*, (Kent, Ohio: Kent State University Press, 1969), 91-95.

Footnotes:

[1] Of course it can be argued exposure (as hypothermia) is the major cause of death for anyone luckly enough to reach a liferaft or lifeboat.

[2] Some sources list him as "Neale."

MAPLEHURST -
"JUMP, DAMN IT JUMP!"

The weather off Lake Superior's Keweenaw on November 30, 1922, was truly terrible. Surf pounding against the north shore was reported by the Eagle Harbor Coast Guard as, "very high" the most severe rating available on the official form. The northwest wind was screaming at 60 miles per hour plus and a blizzard of heavy wet snow blanketed the beach and deep into the woods. By any standard, it was a bad time to be out on the lake.

At 10:35 p.m. Surfman Thomas. W. Bennetts, the Coast Guard lookout at Portage Coast Guard Station, *thought* he saw a steamer that *might* be showing distress signals. The night was utterly black and flying scud and spray from the storm reduced visibility even more. Unsure of what he saw, or *thought* he saw, he called the Boatswain Mate in charge (bo's'un) Charles A. Tucker who was sleeping soundly in his bunk. Rubbing sleep from his eyes, 53-year old Tucker fought through the storm to reach the tower and climb the icy steps to the lookout. Together they determined they couldn't see any distress signals from what was certainly a steamer but it did look suspicious. After a few long minutes the strange ship disappeared from view.

The Coast Guard Station, which was the old Life-Saving Service Station, was located just inside of the "Upper" or west entrance of the Keweenaw Ship Canal (aka Portage Canal). The 27 mile long

NOVEMBER: THE CRUELEST MONTH

The Portage Coast Guard Station at the north entrance to the Portage Lake Ship Canal. The lookout tower is visible in the center of the photo. Author Collection

canal was cut through the base of the Peninsula in the 1860s allowing ships to avoid rounding the ever-dangerous Keweenaw Point in stormy weather. It was an ideal location for the station, the lookout tower offering a commanding view of Superior and allowing the crew to launch their boats into the calm water of the canal before dashing out into the lake for a rescue. The original Life-Saving Station was established in 1885.

Tucker had a feeling they would see the unknown steamer again. Previously, he was the Keeper of the Eagle Harbor Life-Saving Service Station. When the old Life-Saving Service and Revenue Marine were combined in 1915 to form the Coast Guard, the "Keepers" were all converted to "Boatswain's Mates." The crews though continued to be called "Surfmen" and retained the unique numbering system, at least for a while. Surfmen were numbered 1 - 8 beginning with the most senior and 8 the least. Tucker was very experienced with shipwrecks. In fact, he and his entire Eagle Harbor crew received Gold Life-Saving Medals for their part in rescuing the crew of the big freighter *L.C. Waldo*, a victim of the infamous November 1913, storm. The Portage Life-Saving crew also participated in the rescue and both received Gold Medals making it only the second time in the 44-year history of Service two crews received medals for the same rescue. The medals are extremely prestigious and very rarely awarded. Tucker was one of a special and rare breed of men. His Number 3 Surfmen, Oscar Marshall, was the Number 7 at Portage during the *Waldo* rescue and also a medal holder. The lookout, Thomas W. Bennetts, was the old Number 2 at Eagle Harbor and another medal awardee. By any standard, Tucker's crew was experienced and capable of whatever tasks were required. Considering the situation, Tucker ordered the 36-foot motor lifeboat readied for use... just in case.

Tucker remained in the lookout tower with Bennetts until midnight watching for the mysterious steamer before returning to his quarters. Only minutes later, Bennetts spotted a small steamer about four miles northwest of the station. She was making very heavy weather of the storm. He kept his eye on her until she was west of the lookout tower. At 12:50 a.m. she began burning flares and blowing distress blasts with her steam whistle. Now it was time for action and he quickly sounded the alarm!

At 1:00 a.m. the big motor lifeboat rumbled down the launchway and into the canal. Ahead, just past the entrance breakwaters, the wild lake waited. With the old bo's'un at the wheel and his six-man crew

Nine years before the Maplehurst *wreck Tucker and his Portage Lake crew were awarded Gold Life-Saving Medals for their role in the rescue of the crew of the steamer* L.C. Waldo *on Keweenaw Point. Although some of the crew had changed since then, several remained, providing a core of skill and courage.* Author Collection

holding on, the lifeboat cleared the powerful currents and tumbling waves at the canal entrance. This wasn't one of the 36-footers that would gain fame as perhaps the finest coastal motor lifeboats in the world.[1] They didn't come into service until 1929.

Instead, the Portage boat was a 36-foot "Type H" issued to the station earlier in the year. She was a well-built and capable motor lifeboat having a carvel hull with a inch and a half cypress planks. Self-bailing, she also had four thwarts for eight oars as a back up to her gasoline engine. Full speed was 9.2 knots and range 275 miles. One design flaw involved the steering wheel. Place aft of the motor compartment, it had no windscreen to protect the coxswain from driving spray or sleet. "Conning" the boat in heavy weather was more difficult than it needed to be. She replaced *Champion*, the station's old 1910 model Type E, also a 36-footer. The old lifesavers had the tradition of naming their lifeboats, a custom the new Coast Guard soon banished in favor of impersonal numbers.

Forty-five minutes after launching Tucker and his crew reached the steamer, now identified as the *Maplehurst*.

The 36-foot motor lifeboat was key to the Maplehurst *rescue. Don Nelson Collection*

The 243-foot steamer Maplehurst *was built in 1892 as the* Cadillac. *Author Collection*

When the Coast Guardsmen hauled up to her, the steamer was about two miles out and four miles west of the canal and heading into the seas under her own power but making no progress. In the words of Tucker, "the waves were sweeping her from stem to stern and demolishing her upper works."

Since it was obvious to Tucker she would never survive the storm he decided to start the rescue immediately. Running up her lee side he yelled through his megaphone directing the steamer's crew to stand by to jump into the lifeboat when he came around again.

Timing his turn carefully in the crashing seas, Tucker came about and ran close in to the *Maplehurst*. But no one jumped! He repeated the difficult maneuver three times but the steamer's crew stayed aboard. On the fourth try, one man finally leaped into the lifeboat. He then told Tucker the crew was afraid to abandon ship, the captain having told them no small boat could possibly survive the breaking waves!

The fifth time Tucker came alongside, three more crewmembers tumbled aboard. But the banshee winds had been blowing the *Maplehurst* toward the canal breakwaters at a very fast pace. The time left to get the crew off was critically short. Another pass and another man jumped but missed the lifeboat and drowned before the Surfmen could drag him aboard. It was the mate Henry J. Smith.

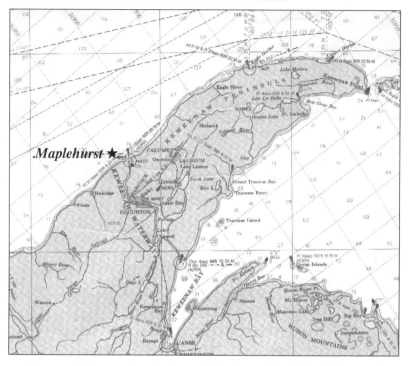

Time and time again Tucker skillfully guided his lifeboat close along side the dying steamer. A single misjudgment of wind or sea and the frail craft would have been smashed to pieces against the steel hull. The Coast Guard motor lifeboat Tucker was using was a remarkably strong and seaworthy craft, soon to develop into one of the finest coastal rescue craft in the world but no wood boat could survive being battered against a steel hull and that was the danger Tucker and his men were facing each time they ran alongside the steamer. To help control the lifeboat in the powerful seas Tucker used two trusted men at the wheel bar.

In spite of Tucker's repeated calls for the remaining men to jump, no more did until his tenth pass when five more tumbled into the lifeboat. It was his last pass. The steamer was now too close to the deadly rock breakwater. Her engine was dead and she lay broadside to the seas, drifting toward certain destruction. Tucker could no longer slip his lifeboat in the lee between ship and shore.

Ominously, the lifeboat engine began to miss! As close as he was to the breakers smashing into shore and breakwater, it was a serious problem. If the engine quit the lifeboat and all aboard was going into the breakers with deadly results. With little choice he nursed the coughing engine and headed further out into the lake.

At this point, a tremendous wave slammed into the steamer, carrying away the rest of her upper works and snuffing out her lights. She was a dead ship. Driven fast by the thundering waves, she grounded hard in the shallow water just off the breakers. The pounding surf had no mercy on the steamer as it methodically beat her to pieces. Minus the steamer's lights to guide him and blinded by the thick snow, Tucker lost sight of the *Maplehurst* in the Stygian blackness.

With his engine running a bit smoother, Tucker headed back for the station arriving at 2:50 a.m. Only nine shivering survivors were aboard his lifeboat. Had the rest of the crew followed his instructions and jumped, certainly more would have lived. Instead, ten men died. After providing the survivors with dry clothing from the Blue Anchor Society box, and assuring they were cared for, Tucker left one man at the station and put his crew to work patrolling the beach opposite the wreck, prepared to assist if by some miracle a sailor reached shore alive. When the dim gray dawn finally came what was left of the *Maplehurst* was clearly visible above the seas; a thin ribbon of broken hull, a smokestack and two derrick cranes. Everything else was gone! She was a mere 200 feet from the west breakwater.

Maplehurst crewman Harry Murphy, working in the engineroom, later related his take on the disaster (although the comments have likely been "wordsmithed" by a journalist). "At 11:30 I was awakened by a distress signal and excited voices in the boiler room. I scrambled to the deck and saw a monstrous wave go over the ship, men running up and down the deck and at times clinging to the bridge to prevent their being swept into the raging sea. About 12:30 a big wave swept away the bridge and damaged the cabin. Captain Menard, the Chief Engineer, the cook and I crawled into the cabin where we were tossed around and thrown violently to the floor time and time again."

During the following days the patrolling Coast Guardsmen recovered many of the bodies of the men who decided to stay aboard. Had they but listened to the veteran Life-Saver, they all would likely have lived.

The engine problem in the motor lifeboat was no fluke. She likely had a 36 horsepower Gray-Prior, which tended to wear out quickly.

NOVEMBER: THE CRUELEST MONTH

Since it was a hazard for navigation, the Army Corp of Engineers had to dynamite the wreckage. Author Collection

The crew was evidently having trouble with it for some time since on December 6 they received a new Wisconsin motor to replace it. Considering the tremendous battering the little lifeboat was taking, keeping any engine running, especially one with a gravity-fed fuel supply, was a minor miracle.

The 243-foot *Maplehurst* was built by the Chicago Shipbuilding Company in 1892 as the *Cadillac* for the Cleveland Cliffs Iron Company. She was smaller than CCI's normal vessels since the company thought it necessary to be able to ship beyond Lake Erie through the Welland Canal and St. Lawrence. However, the iron ore trade from Lake Superior to the Lake Erie mills increased so quickly trading further east wasn't necessary and she became excess to the fleet. J.W. Norcross Company purchased her in 1912 and in 1920 she was sold to Canada Steamship Lines (CSL) and renamed. The CSL policy at the time was to name all ships with the prefix "MAPLE" and all steel hull ships with a suffix beginning with "H." Thus was born the *Maplehurst*.

She was upbound for Fort William (today's Thunder Bay) from Lorain, Ohio on Lake Erie with 1,800 tons of coal when the storm

Little was left of the steamer following the lake's assault. K.E. Thro Collection

The wreck was later dynamited as a danger to navigation. Author Collection

slammed into her. She reached a point just southeast of Isle Royale when 29-year old Captain Nelson G. Menard, one of the youngest captains in the CSL fleet, decided not to buck head on into the storm any longer but to run to shelter at the Keweenaw. He intended to take cover in the canal but a few miles off the entrance the ship gave signs of breaking up. At that point he started firing distress flares and signals.

Part of the problem the *Maplehurst* likely encountered in trying to go into the canal was the narrow entrance. There wasn't any room for error. Even experienced captains had trouble in good conditions. It the midst of a storm, blinded by snow and hoping to enter a canal never entered before would be a real challenge. Since the pierhead light was knocked out by the storm, he was trying to find a black canal in a black peninsula in a black night in the midst of a storm, his challenge was nearly impossible to meet.

The *Maplehurst/Cadillac* was not an especially lucky ship. In 1912 she sank in the Bay of Quinte on Lake Ontario after striking some pilings. Later she collided with the steamer *Leigh* in the Welland Canal.

Although the famous wrecker Tom Reid looked the *Maplehurst* wreck over closely, even he admitted she was too far-gone for salvage. Finally, the remains were dynamited as a hazard to navigation.[i]

References:

Dana Thomas Bowen, *Shipwrecks of the Great Lakes* (Cleveland: Freshwater Press, 1952), 285-292.

Duluth News-Tribune, December 1, 10, 1922.

John O. Greenwood, *The Fleet Histories Series, Volume VI* (Cleveland: Freshwater Press, 1998), 4-5. 91.

John O. Greenwood, *Namesakes 1920-1929* (Cleveland: Freshwater Press, 1984), 48.

"Log of Coast Guard Station No. 300 (Portage) November 30, December 1 - 7, 1922" RG 26, NARA.

Frederick W. Mikko, "The Choice of the Crew of the *Maplehurst*,"

Inland Seas, Fall 1987, 164-167.

Runge Collection, Milwaukee Public Library.

Robert L. Scheina, *U.S. Coast Guard Cutters and Craft of World War II* (Annapolis: U.S. Naval Institute Press, 1982), 257.

Peter Van der Linden, *Great Lakes Ships We Remember, Volume II* (Cleveland: Freshwater Press, 1979) 205-206.

William D. Wilkerson and Commander Timothy R. Dring, USNR (Retired), *American Coastal Rescue Craft, A Design History of Coastal Rescue Craft Used by the United States Life-Saving Service and United States Coast Guard* - CD Media (Gainesville: University Press of Florida, 2009), 28, 35-36.

Footnotes:

[i] Captain W. F. Amsbary, *The Sailing Career of Captain W. F. Amsbary* (unpublished manuscript - Stonehouse Collection), 4-5:

[1] "T" Class followed by the "TR" and "TRS"

ANNA C. MINCH, WILLIAM D. DAVOCK AND NOVADOC - ARMISTICE DAY 1940-WHEN DEATH CAME IN BUNCHES

Storm

There are three storms generally recognized as vying for the title of the "worst" to ever pummel the Great Lakes; November 27-28, 1905, November 6-9, 1913 and November 11, 1940. All have their own supporters who can cite wind speeds, wave height, number of ships wrecked and sailors killed. But since the storms occurred during somewhat different historical periods reflecting changes in ship design and operation and centered to a degree on different geographic areas as well as the pure randomness of chance; where what ship is when it struck and the variability of fortune, determining which was the "worst" is a fool's game. Suffice it to be agreed they were all stem-winders of rare devastation!

The 1940 Armistice Day storm certainly belongs among this trio of death.[1] It began with mild weather ahead of an intense low pressure system tracking from Kansas to western Wisconsin, quickly followed by a furious blizzard. The severity of the storm and plunging temperatures caught many people off-guard. During the morning of November 11, temperatures reached 60 degrees but by the following morning plummeted to single digit readings. Such deep cold and heavy snow were very unusual for this early in the season. Minnesota received up to 26 inches of snow and Wisconsin was lashed with winds of 50 to 80 mph as well as deep snow over parts of Wisconsin, South Dakota, Nebraska, Minnesota, Iowa and Michigan. The extreme wind built snowdrifts 20 feet high, in some places burying highways, streets and railroads. Thousands of cattle and poultry froze to death. Officials blamed the storm for 144 fatalities including 13 in Wisconsin, most of which were duck hunters along the Mississippi River and reputedly another 49 in Minnesota, 14 in Illinois and four in Michigan and two near Windsor, Ontario. The hunters went out dressed for warm weather and the sudden onslaught of cold caught them unprepared. The high wind whipped up lakes and rivers to the point they couldn't escape to the mainland. They literally died in their hunting stands, in some instances later found frozen stiff as their decoys. Stories are told of great flocks of ducks driven east just ahead of the rapidly moving storm system. Awed by sudden abundance of targets, hunters who should have run to safety stayed to enjoy the best shooting of their lives, throwing huge amounts of lead in the air. It was also the last shooting in their lives!

The testimony of a 17-year old survivor is especially poignant. The young hunter, his father, Carl; 16-year old brother, Raymond; and a friend, Bill, were all caught along the Mississippi when the weather curtain dropped. Just imagine the horror this teenager endured! "Bill kept falling asleep and we had to hit him to keep him awake. He died about 2 o'clock in the morning. At 11:00 a.m. my brother died and dad died about three hours later. I sat on a stump and held my dog until about 2:30 when I saw a boat coming to get me. I don't remember any more."

In weather terms much of the devastation was caused by a secondary disturbance from the one whose high winds collapsed the famous Tacoma Narrows bridge ("Galloping Gertie") on November 7. The little brother system developed inland and moved southeastward, crossing the Rocky Mountains, curving eastward over the southern Great Plains and north-northeastward across the extreme Upper Great Lakes. At 9:00 a.m. on November 10 the first front boiled into Chicago shifting the wind from southeast to southwest. Two and a half hours later, the major front came through with a wind rapidly increasing to 65 mph. For ships on the lake, it had now "hit the fan!"

Milwaukee only received a trace of snow, but 80-mph winds downed hundreds of trees. Detroit was hammered, too. The 733-foot high WJR radio transmitter tower, the tallest structure in Michigan, toppled in winds gusting to 78-mph. In the hinterlands telephone and power lines were knocked down everywhere isolating many communities and roads blocked by hundreds of downed trees. Grand Rapids, Michigan, was battered by 80-mph winds. The St. Clair River, the major shipping artery between Lake Huron and the Detroit River dropped two and a half feet when the wind literally blew the water back into Lake Huron. The lightship anchored at the Port Huron end of the river was struck so hard by the wind she dragged her massive mushroom anchors 4,000 feet out of position. On the open lake water was pushed back so far northward Saginaw Bay was emptied for a mile! Freighters in the Detroit River doubled or tripled their moorings to hold fast to their docks.

Water in Chicago dropped over four and a half feet and rose the same amount at Beaver Island in the northern lake. It was literally blown from one end to the other.

Weather forecasting of the storm's arrival was abysmal. For shipmasters and public alike it was a haymaker seemingly coming out of nowhere.

Lake Michigan received the brunt of the shipping damage. For example, Lansing Shoals Light in the northern lake recorded winds of 126-miles per hour. The shoals are about four and a half miles northeast of Squaw Island, at the northern end of a narrow passage between the Straits and the northern harbors of Lake Michigan and Green Bay. It is a major danger to any ship unfamiliar with the details of the passage. The "Art Deco" style lighthouse was first illuminated in October 1928. Prior to then a lightship warned mariners from danger. The storm coated the light with an estimated seven inches of ice and blew out most of the viewports sending civilian Keepers G. L. Gordon and W. L. Keller to shelter in an inner room deep within the concrete crib. Mountainous waves battered the light and thick snow obscured the beacon from mariners, making it nothing more than a big ice covered concrete hazard to navigation. That the lighthouse withstood such pounding is testimony to the design and strength of construction.

Vessel captains in 1940 essentially relied on three sources for weather information; marine radio stations like the Lorain Radio in Lorain, Ohio, public commercial stations (most captains had a radio of some sort in their cabin) and experience. The first two failed utterly to warn of the storm. The third was perhaps most successful but in a limited fashion. Captains who kept a wary eye on their trusty "glass" knew weather was coming when they saw the mercury plummet but how bad it would be and for how long was a guess. For a time prior to 1940 there was an experiment involving Coast Guard stations providing weather forecasts to commercial ships. According to old time captains it failed when it became too difficult for the Coast Guard to actually provide the forecast. It seems the freighter captain would radio in and ask for the information and the Coast Guardsmen on radio watch would reply to wait; he had to find someone else. Tired of the needless delay the freighters just stopped calling, defeated by government inefficiency.

The Ships

Lake Michigan

While the Armistice Day storm is usually thought of in terms strictly of the fates of three ships, the *William B. Davock*, *Anna C. Minch* and *Novadoc*, there were other, ultimately luckier ships that survived although battered and beaten.

Northern Lake Michigan saw the steamer 343-foot *Frank J. Peterson* with a cargo of scrap steel ashore on St. Helena Island. A Coast Guard 36-foot motor lifeboat with a crew of four battled her way out to the ship to make certain the sailors aboard were safe. The Coast Guard 36 boat remains one of the finest coastal rescue craft ever built but it took remarkable courage to make the long and dangerous run to the *Peterson*.

The 369-foot car ferry *City Of Flint* 32 missed the piers trying to enter the harbor at Ludington at 7:00 p.m. on November 10, grounding hard in the shallow water 800-feet off the beach. The local Coast Guard crew used their Lyle gun and breeches buoy to remove two of the crew suffering from exposure. When it was apparent she

The big carferry City Of Flint *was blown into the shallows at Ludington, Michigan. Author Collection*

wasn't going to pieces, the remainder stayed aboard. Since the ship was still "live" in the waves, properly tensioning the hawser to keep the men above the water was nearly impossible, resulting in the two mostly being dragged through the surf to the beach. If they weren't suffering from exposure before, they surely were afterward! She was recovered several days later without serious damage.

Other ships battled through the storm. The 589-foot Pittsburg steamer *Thomas F. Cole* is characteristic of the freshwater hell raging on the lake. Captain R. W. Parsons took the *Cole* out of Gary, Indiana, at 4:00 p.m. on November 10 bound for the Straits of Mackinac. At the time the wind was 25-mph from the southeast and every indication was for an easy run north. By 10:00 a.m. on the 10th, the wind was blowing a real gagger. The trusty barometer was also falling rapidly indicating the worst was yet to come. He had expected the wind to shift northeast which would have given him a sheltered course under cover of the west Michigan shore. But conditions were so bad Captain Parsons decided to turn and run southwest to shelter.

The *Cole* made good weather of it until a series of enormous waves lifted her bow so high out of the water it presented enough surface area to allow the screaming wind to push her 180-degrees around so she was heading back northeast. Worse, perhaps, the steamer didn't have enough power to turn back on her original course. Regardless of how skillfully he tried, Captain Parsons couldn't bring her around. All he could do was go where the storm wanted him to go. Adding to his misery, the cold air over the relatively warm water caused steam fog to rise off the lake dropping visibility to a couple of hundred feet. This was before the days of radar so the *Cole* was running blind into the massive storm.

Around midnight an enormous wave rose over her stern and swept aboard caving in the steel plating on the aft cabin and ripping out the telephone cables to the stern. The steel lifeline strung between the fore and aft houses had already carried away so there was no way to communicate between the two ends of the ship. Without the lifeline any attempt to pass fore or aft was suicidal in the extreme. In practical terms this also meant the forward crew were unable to get any food or even coffee. For 36 long hours they struggled not only with the wind and waves but with the absence of chow and always critical caffeine.

The crew of the Sinola *required the Coast Guard from Munising, Michigan on Lake Superior to remove them by breeches buoy. Author Collection*

When the storm moderated enough for some of the crew to chance a trip to the galley, they found a scene of utter destruction. The heavy iron stove was broken into bits, oak wall paneling smashed to kindling and deck covered with pots, pans, silverware and shattered dishes and crockery. If it could be broken, it was!

The open weather deck was a foot deep in ice, dangerous in the extreme since it changed the center of gravity. Add enough topside ice and chances of capsizing increased radically.

Ships like the *Cole* typically bend and twist in storm and gale. The flexing can place enormous strain on the rivets holding the hull plates, ribs, frames, etc. together. When the strain becomes too much, the rivets "pop," literally firing off like large bullets. When the *Cole* finally reached Chicago she had so many rivets missing Captain Parsons claimed her hull looked like a giant cribbage board!

The 416-foot sand-sucker *Sinaloa* was blown ashore at Big Bay de Noc in the northern lake on November 12. She had sucked a cargo of sand near Green Island and was heading for Chicago via Death's Door when the storm slammed into her. The thundering seas tore off her rudder and she was helpless, driven before the winds until fetching up in the shallows. Local fishermen took off 22 of the 42 men aboard and a Coast Guard breeches buoy crew from Munising, the remainder.

The 444-foot *Frank Billings* radioed she was in trouble in the northern lake with water in her cargo hold and pilothouse smashed. She eventually made safe anchor off Seul Choix Point ten miles east of Manistique.

The 415-foot *Conneaut* was storm anchored off Naubinway, 40 miles or so west of the Straits of Mackinac. But her anchors dragged in the banshee winds forcing her into shoal water damaging her rudder and propeller.

Fears were initially felt for the 480-foot *Algosteel* but she turned up safe after sheltering at De Tour in the St. Marys River.

The motorship *Mercury* was reported missing but was found safe sheltering in the lee of North Manitou Island. The tanker *Crudoil* was also thought wrecked but staggered into the Sturgeon Bay Canal with six feet of water sloshing in her hold and disabled steering.

Another tanker, the 251-foot *New Haven Socony*, was thought lost especially after an oar, part of a lifeboat marked with her name and

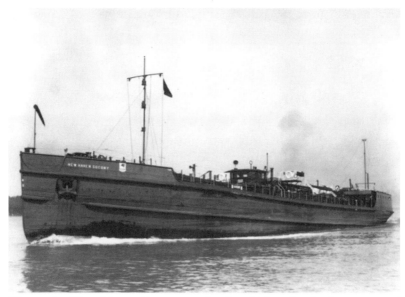

The tanker New Haven Socony *took a fearful beating in the storm and was given up for lost. Author Collection*

pieces of her pilothouse drifted ashore at Grand Haven and an airplane sent to search for her came up empty handed. When she finally arrived at East Chicago covered in a thick layer of shimmering ice it was as if she arose from the dead!

She left East Chicago at 8:45 a.m. on the 11th bound for Muskegon with 600,000 gallons of gasoline. The wind was moderate south-southeast and contrary to the weather report, kept shifting south and westward until around 7:00 p.m. when the storm struck in earnest, blasting hard southwest. At the time, the tanker was about 25 miles southwest of Muskegon.

Ten minutes later a huge wave slammed into the pilothouse and in Captain Harley O. Norton's words, "stove in the after windows on the lower pilothouse, the port side of the upper pilothouse and filled the lower pilothouse with water. The direction finder and the charts that were on the chart table and all the other stuff around was just swept away. The starboard door of the lower pilothouse was knocked off and a couple of men and myself who were there at the time were knocked down. That's when I injured my hand. Incidentally all lights were carried away too; we had no lights except flashlights. We got to the upper pilothouse and I took over the wheel myself. I used a flashlight to see the compass. She started to turn and when she started it was impossible to get her back again. I then came around and headed her into the seas."

"...shortly after I got her straightened out - I saw she was apparently doing better that way, I sent the wheelsman and ordinary seaman down to get dry clothes on. They were just soaking wet..."

"I kept the second mate in the pilothouse with me. After the wheelsman and ordinary seaman got back reporting conditions, the mate and steward came up with a dry jacket for me. As I had injured my hand when the big sea hit us, the mate asked if he couldn't take over to relieve me. I went back and the chief engineer and steward done up my hand and I was just changing my clothes when the mate and the boatswain came back and told me the steering gear was out of commission in the upper pilothouse and the chief and I went back into the steering engine room to arrange controls back there. We knocked out the pins in the shaft and used a small emergency wheel that is used for such purpose. I went up to the top deck and hollered directions down; (author's note - he was giving course directions to the men at the emergency wheel) I also gave explicit orders to the engineers not to touch the throttles unless hearing from me. At that time we were running dead slow - just as slow as she would turn and keep her in the sea. We had no compass or indication equipment of any kind. The only thing I could do under the circumstances was to keep her as near to the sea as she would ride until daylight or when we could see something."

The captain reported waves higher than her 45-foot mast. One lifeboat was swept away and another damaged.

"We continued that way all night and all the next day and all the next night until 5:00 o'clock in the morning; it was a quarter after four to be exact. It was a quarter after four the wind moderated, the sea gone down, but we didn't know our position. I had no idea where I was, I had no lights, but the moon was bright and I did get a sight of the North Star and I knew I was headed in approximately a southwest direction. I stopped the engines at a quarter after four and let her lay until daylight. About a quarter to five I sighted a ship on the horizon, on the port bow and immediately made signals. He came over and I asked him our position."

"It was the steamship *Pan Oil*. He told me my position was six miles north of Waukegan and ten miles offshore. He asked if he could be of any assistance and I told him no, we were all right now." Using a compass salvaged from the upper pilothouse the captain safely brought his ship back to East Chicago! Captain Norton is quoted as saying he didn't think she would stay afloat another hour.

Her boatswain later said, "We've been through hell!" It certainly was not an overstatement of the horrendous conditions she battled through.

The package freighter *Alfred H. Smith* pulled the same trick when she arrived from Detroit at Milwaukee two days overdue. Her cargo of smashed automobiles, refrigerators and cases of sardines and chocolate gave powerful testimony to the ordeal she suffered. Three of the new cars and a truck carried on deck were swept overboard by the waves. Several other cars were literally hanging over the rail.

The Canadian package freighter *Arthur Orr* was solidly aground near Waugoshance Point at the north end of Gray's Reef Passage.

Captain James Larsen with the steamer *Pathfinder* was upbound light from Indiana Harbor to Escanaba for ore when she was slammed by the storm. When she left mid afternoon on the 10th winds were southeast and light. The farther north he went, the worse conditions became. When he finally punched his way to the harbor at Escanaba he dropped both anchors intending to shelter behind Sand Point. He later said, "It was just like if you threw out two matches!" It minutes she was fast on Little Bay de Noc Shoal.

The big steamer *George W. Perkins* had her problems with the storm. Captain William McBeth related she was abreast of Pilot Island in the northern lake when the sea and wind literally turned him around. "I got one blast of wind with an enormous sea picked me up and turned me around. I could not hold her." He eventually managed to anchor behind Garden Island.

Some ships reacted quicker to the storm. The *Saturn* was upbound from Indiana Harbor for the Straits of Mackinac, departing shortly after 3:00 a.m. on the 11th. Captain Ralph Fenton headed her off for the east shore of the lake intending to take her up the Manitou Passage. Perhaps sensing something was wrong, at 6:00 a.m. he was thinking of breakfast when he tapped the glass in his cabin and the mercury dropped instead of holding steady. Forgoing chow he went into the pilothouse and told the third mate on watch to contact radio station KDA in Chicago and find out the weather in Madison, Wisconsin. He knew the weather in Madison and Lacrosse would soon be on the lake and wanted to be prepared for it. While he watched, his glass continued to fall and his suspicions increased with every millibar drop. Old time captains learned long before to trust their glass!

When the wind shifted strong out of the south shortly before noon he had enough and swung the *Saturn* direct to the Wisconsin shore. He knew what was coming. He had received no reports of any kind indicating big trouble was coming. Weather in Madison didn't yet change but he knew he needed shelter from the west soon. Asked about it later he just said, "We had a merry old time getting across the lake. The best she would do was holding her into the wind as close as we could get her. That may sound funny but never the less it is true other wise she would throw her wheel (authors note - out of the water). She went along like a sail boat." All the while they were in "blinding snow, you could not see the after end most of the time. Blinding snow and frozen sleet off the water, picked up the crest of the waves off and drove them into us." Shortly after 11:00 p.m. he

The fishing tub Indian *was lost with all five hands. Author Collection*

139

was off Two Rivers, Wisconsin. He turned north and finally anchored for shelter behind St. Martin Island. He didn't make it unscathed, losing three channel irons off the hatches, deck lights and smashed view ports.

The South Haven fishing tugs *Indian* with five men aboard and the *Richard H.* with a crew of three both were lost with all hands.[2] Two more men perished with the motor cruiser *Nancy Jane* in the southern lake.

Lake Superior

Shipping on Lake Superior escaped the worst of the storm. The steamer *Sparta* was thrown on the rocks five miles east of Munising without loss of life. The *Crescent City* (recovered from her sojourn on the rocks on the North Shore from the November 1905, storm)

The Sparta *was pushed into the deadly cliffs of the Pictured Rocks on Lake Superior.* Rutherford B. Hayes Library

was badly beat-up, losing a number of her deck cargo of cars overboard. Captain Harold McCool stated it was, "…the worst storm on the Great Lakes in 40 years," and "…more severe than the disastrous storm during the fall of 1913 (November 1913)."

A large number of freighters sheltered in the St. Marys River rather than either punch off into Superior or Huron. At least 25 boats were anchored near the De Tour Coal Dock. The waves were pounding into the river so strongly from the south, a number of boats downstream hauled anchor and went deeper upstream.

Lake Huron

Shipping in Lake Huron largely escaped from storm damage. The steamer *Wyandotte*, inbound to Alpena with coal was an exception, seas breaking over her decks sending water pouring down her stack and wreaking havoc topside.

Erie-Ontario

Lakes Erie and Ontario were too far from the storm's center and escaped with only minor damages. Once in a while a weather bullet is dodged and that's what happened in 1940.

Regardless of the general carnage, the 1940 Armistice Day storm is often remembered only in terms of three Lake Michigan shipwrecks; the *William D. Davock*, *Anna C. Minch* and *Novadoc*.

William D. Davock

The 420-foot *William B. Davock* was upbound for Chicago with coal under command of Captain Charles W. Allen of Detroit. She carried a crew of 32 and was owned by Pickands, Mather and Company (Interlake Steamship Company) of Cleveland. Built in 1907 by the Great Lakes Engineering Works for the Vulcan Steamship Company, she was a one of a kind design having no identical sisters. She joined the Pickands, Mather fleet in 1915 and was rebuilt in 1923. Pickands, Mather ran the second largest fleet on the lakes at the time. Only the Pittsburg Fleet (U.S. Steel) was bigger.

The steamer William B. Davock *at the Soo. Author Collection*

She was typical of the vessels used in the iron, grain and coal trade. Normal speed was 11 1/2 miles per hour. Navigation was via gyro, true and magnetic compasses, radio direction finder and ship to shore radio. The radiotelephone was located in the pilothouse with an extension in the captain's cabin. And of course there was always the tried and true taffrail log.

The *Davock's* last trip started innocently enough. She left Erie, Pennsylvania around noon on the 10th after loading 7,241 short tons of coal at the P. and E. Coal Dock, passing through the Straits of Mackinac in company with the steamer *Dalwarnic*.[3] She was by no means over loaded but rather filled to her winter draft marks (aka

Plimsol mark).[4] Since the winds were blowing southeasterly it is assumed she followed the east shore of the lake as would be common under the circumstance. This would have brought her down through the narrow Gray's Reef Passage into the Manitou Passage along the lake's east coast in relatively sheltered waters.

Her last known direct contact with anyone was at 7:30 a.m. on November 11 when her captain radioed the company in Cleveland that he was a dozen miles west of Ludington, wind east-southeast, fresh and hazy and all was well. At 4:00 a.m. she spoke with the steamer *Pathfinder* reporting she was ten miles off Big Sable reporting very strong east-southeast winds but, "he was going along nicely and making good weather." The captain of the *Pathfinder* remembered the forecast called for shifting northwest but there was no mention of gales. He did note his glass was falling and experience telling him a storm "was brewing."

The freighter *P.E. Crowley* northbound from South Chicago with general freight spotted the *Davock* running southward at 8:00 a.m. on the 11th. Captain Albert Hayden spoke with his third mate over the likelihood the *Davock* would soon be turning north but if so it would be a short respite since both were certain the winds would clock around to the southwest.

When the wind shifted strong southwest the *Davock* was in a precarious position close by a lee shore without the power to claw her way off. As the hurricane like winds increased they built up monstrous seas, too large for the 33-year old freighter to battle through.

Why she never radioed a distress call or even reported her situation is unknown. Perhaps the antenna blew away, or radio shorted out when a pilothouse window blew out sending a deluge of water into the cabin. She also could have radioed and never been heard. The best we can do is guess.

Alone she would have fought a desperate battle with the lake. Great waves sweeping over her spar deck, hammering water into every weak point, smashing hatches, doorways, windows and portholes; wave after wave attacking her, each seemingly bent on her destruction. Her best hope was to find shelter but she was on the wrong side of the lake. The only potential harbors of refuge were Manistee, Muskegon and Frankfort. All were virtually impossible to enter under such horrendous storm conditions with narrow channels

NOVEMBER: THE CRUELEST MONTH

The Davock *at an unloading dock. Author Collection*

running between rock breakwaters. With the wind and sea screaming from the south it would have been impossible to line up with the entrance and hold her straight. While Frankfort was a major car ferry terminal even the highly skilled and experienced ferry captains wouldn't make the attempt when the lake was howling as she was. She could have tried to run back north and laid in behind one of the Manitou Islands but making a 180-degree turn was impossible given the horrendous conditions. She just didn't have the power in her old engines to drive her bow around against the force of wind and wave. Perhaps she did try to turn only to capsize in the attempt.

There was later speculation she could have collided with the *Minch*. It is hard to conceive of such an accident, two ships smashing together in the midst of the lake, but stranger collisions have happened so marine men considered it possible.

Two of the *Davock's* metal lifeboats with four dead sailors aboard, came ashore about four and a half miles south of Ludington. They were the first clues to the missing steamer. The starboard side of the number one boat was crumpled, perhaps from battering against the hull of the steamer. The steamer's message case was found near the lifeboats. It was empty save for the 1929 crew list. Many freighters carried waterproof brass tubes in the pilothouse. They were intended to provide a safe container for a last message to those ashore when the ship was sinking assuming the captain remembered to toss it overboard or if floated free when the ship sank. Or, of course, remembered to actually put a message into it. Based on the 1929 crew list, evidently no captain had opened it since 1929!

In a desperate effort to find their missing steamer, or at least the wreck thereof, the Pickands, Mather chartered an airplane to search for her. It was a fruitless effort.

None of the reported 14 bodies recovered from the *Davock* were greatly injured. The coroner simply listing the cause of death as, "expired from shipwreck." Eleven of the crewmen wore life jackets, including all three mates. Clearly the men knew the ship was sinking and made some effort to survive. Assuming the lifeboats were launched as opposed to breaking off when she plunged for the bottom or swept away by boarding seas, it shows a deliberate effort to abandon ship. Launching a lifeboat in a storm is an incredibly difficult task. The four sailors found in the lifeboat reinforce the concept of a deliberate decision.

Rudder damage as the cause of loss was considered unlikely during the subsequent Coast Guard investigation. The Chief Engineer of the company said her steering engine was a Williamson screw type installed on a number of vessels in their fleet and that captains and engineers were "very taken up with it." One old captain related the steering gear was one of a kind and, "the best we have." He described it as, "old schooner equipment" that someone sold to the builder but she was a "dandy" and "the best."

The Chief also felt it very unlikely her steering failed during the storm. Obviously any steering failure could be deadly. He explained the motion of the steering wheel was transmitted by a shaft with a drum on the end of it running straight from the pilothouse. In turn half inch steel cables from the drum ran aft to the steering engine. To protect the cables from jamming the ferrules were sealed and mounted away from the cargo. To assure the cables are in first class condition company policy was to check them after every trip.

The engine room and associated equipment were considered in first class condition and no problems were reported prior to her last trip.

NOVEMBER: THE CRUELEST MONTH

A previous *Davock's* captain, 52- year-old Alfred C. Drouillard also testified at the Coast Guard investigation. Drouillard had wide experience, holding his license since 1914. At the time of his testimony he was captain of the 600-foot *Charles M. Schwab*. He related when he sailed the *Davock* in 1934 and 1935 he, "considered her a good boat, very good hull." But he hedged a bit stating, "she had power enough, as much as most boats carry on the lakes."

Questioned on the weather, Drouillard said he was downbound from Superior to Indiana Harbor with ore when he received his update from Lorain Radio at 10 p.m. on the 10th saying fresh southeast wind shifting northeast. He saw it as nothing extraordinary for that time of year. By 8 p.m. on the 11th he was in mid lake somewhere off Sheboygan, Wisconsin, and being blasted by 90 mile per hour winds. Estimating one squall at over 100-mph. Several other captains claimed gusts of 120 miles per hour. The seas were monstrous and in Drouillard's words, "I think 40% bigger than anything I ever experienced in my life" and "...twice as high as any I have seen before." Considering the captain was a 37-year Lakes veteran, it was an amazing evaluation of the storm.

In spite of the severity of the storm, Drouillard and the *Schwab* came through will little damage, amounting to having a broken after cabin door. He claimed he knew no reason, "why the *Davock* should not have come through. She is a good boat and well equipped, her hull was a very good hull."

When pressed for his opinion of what caused the disaster, the captain could only relate, "I think it is one of those things. Something happened is all. We don't know what happened, I would not even make a guess, the *Davock* was as good a boat I ever rode on."

Captain Luke J. Lavely of Marine City, Michigan, came out of retirement with several other veteran masters to captain the *Davock* for the fall of 1939. "When the company brought the boats out in the fall they didn't want the younger captains to drive them in the fall but instead to have experienced men do the job," "when the gales of November come calling." (Author's comment.)

Hatch covers are long considered a weakness for Great Lakes freighters. During Coast Guard testimony Lavely was careful to explain how the steamer's hatch system worked. She had 12 hatches on 24-foot centers, three each for each of her four cargo holds. Each hatch was about ten feet by four feet, the coamings 15 inches amidships sloping to 12 inches.

Her hatch covers were the Mullholland type, a series of overlapping three-eighths inch steel plates designed to seal the holds from flooding seas. The individual plates were fastened with 26 special screws tightened with large wrenches as well as steel pins through the leaves and coaming. Each side of the *Davock* hatch covers had five leaves for a total of ten across the entire hatch. To assure the hatches were well protected heavy tarpaulins were added on top and secured in place with steel bars. The tarpaulins actually didn't make the hatches waterproof but rather allowed them to shed water easier. Captain Lavely claimed he never had any trouble with his hatches in a seaway.

During questioning it was revealed the *Davock* also had two scuttle hatches through the maindeck, one between hold one and two and the second between three and four. Made of half inch thick steel the scuttle hatches were designed to allow access to the cargo hold without having to open the main hatches. They were secured with dogs that fit into deck slots. A rubber gasket served to make them waterproof from boarding waves. In addition she had a coalbunker hatch on top of the aft cabin forward of the smokestack. The hatch was used to load coal directly into her coalbunker for feeding the boilers. The steel cover was held in place with two heavy steel bars. Doubtless though the bunker hatch wasn't secured to the same standard as the deck hatches which would face the greater hazard from boarding seas. There is in fact some question whether the bunker hatch was secured at all. When she left the P. and E. Dock the dock foreman recalled the bunker coal was piled so high the hatch covers could not be secured.[5]

Captain Lavely also strongly endorsed the seaworthiness of the *Davock* saying, "I have sailed many boats in 36 years. I figured she was the stoutest little boat that I have been on." He also related she wasn't a "wet" ship either. When coming down on Lake Superior with a 50-60 mile an hour north wind she was "on top all of the time. There were other ships with us and their decks were washed all the time."

Lavely had long experience with storms on the lakes, having survived the infamous 1905 and 1913 "blows." He knew what he was talking about.

Fleet captain Zealand was very proud of the *Davock* saying, "That little boat should weather anything the other boats did." When pressed for an explanation of loss, the best he could offer was, "He may have dropped down (authors note - into the "hole" behind an especially large wave) until he hit bottom and one end stayed down and the sea picked the other end up." He also ventured an opinion on the rumor she was trying to reach Grand Haven saying she, "…would not have had a Chinaman's chance anymore than the *City Of Flint* had going into port. He goes in every day and sometimes twice a day." By contrast had the *Davock* been on the west side of the lake Chicago, South Chicago, Sheboygan and Manitowoc all offered good and accessible shelter.[6]

Her deck officers were well experienced having been with the Pickands, Mather fleet for years as was her chief engineer. None were obvious weak links.

Anna C. Minch

The 380-foot *Anna C. Minch* operated by the Sarnia Steamship Company was also bound for Chicago with coal and passed through the Straits four hours after the *Davock*. She would have followed the same routing as the *Davock*, down Gray's Reef Passage and the Manitou Passage, emerging in the open lake just north of Point Betsie. And she would have been slammed by the same monstrous waves and banshee winds.

The *Minch* was built in 1903 in Cleveland by the American Shipbuilding Company for the Kinsman Transit Company. She was sold Canadian in 1926.

Initially the company thought the *Minch* safe but when the bodies of her crew began to drift ashore at Ludington it was stark proof of her loss and the death of the 24 men aboard.

Patrols regularly scanned the beaches looking for bodies from both vessels. They were often rewarded. About half of the bodies of the *Davock* crew were eventually found in the Pentwater area and others near Ludington. The men came in amidst the flotsam of shipwreck; a clutter of life rings, broken lifeboats, oars, tarpaulins, cabin doors, fragments of furniture, all telling the chilling story of death on the

The Anna Minch. *Author Collection*

lake. Marine men thought many of the victims would never be found, their remains trapped forever inside their ships.

Searching for the bodies coming ashore wasn't just a job for the Coast Guard. A detachment of 25 men from the Civilian Conservation Corps at Camp Ludington-Pere Marquette trekked the sandy beach from Muskegon north to Big Point Sable. Many of the remains were taken to local funeral homes and to a temporary morgue established in the Salvation Army building.

Three that were unidentified were eventually interred in Ludington's Lakeview Cemetery including one from the *Minch*. The remaining bodies were shipped home to loved ones.

The general locations where the bodies from the *Davock* and *Minch* were discovered provided a pointer to where the wrecks where, the *Davock's* being found generally 15 miles further north than those from the *Minch*.

When the *Minch* wreck was discovered on November 15 by Clyde Cross (More about Cross later in this chapter), she was in a mere 40 feet of water 1.7 miles, 216 degrees from the pier head in Pentwater. Her mast was sticking up above the surface! Cross later told a reporter he just went out, "to see what he could see." What he at first thought was just a seagull sitting on the water turned out to be the tip of the mast with a small pennant still attached.

When the first hardhat divers from the salvage tug *Tee Zee Lee* of Muskegon initially examined the wreck he reported it was only the front half of the vessel and pilothouse and forward cabin were missing. He also stated the hull was broken from the spar deck where the number one hatch should be "clean down to the turn of the bilge." The plates were turned inward at the front part of the hole while the back was jagged. The break wasn't vertical but instead on a 45-degree angle. On the opposite or starboard side the hull plates were rolled in and practically flat. The stern was later found nearby but offered no clear answers to the loss.

Since the *Davock's* hull was still missing and the bodies of both crews were partially intermingled on the beach, marine men theorized the two ships collided during the height of the storm. Since they were of the same general vintage, construction and power, it is fair to assume they would have experienced the same plummeting.

The problem in tying the collision theory together was the timing. Since the *Minch* was four hours behind the *Davock* there could have been a separation of as much as 40 miles. How could the ships have come together?

The Minch *was typical of many of the ships on the Lakes when she started her career.* Author Collection

ANNA C. MINCH, WILLIAM D. DAVOCK & NOVADOC

Although seaworthy the Minch *was an "old-timer" in 1940. Author Collection*

The *Minch* would have had to pass the *Davock*, then perhaps become disabled, lose her wheel or rudder or otherwise unable to make progress. Drifting out of control and likely in the trough of the seas, she was suddenly rammed by the *Davock* appearing unexpectedly out of the dark storm. While certainly unlikely, it is possible and would neatly explain the intermixed bodies and *Minch* hull damage. But of course it is only a theory.

Another explanation postulated during the height of the storm the *Minch* suddenly breaks in two. As the forward section falls away the stern briefly continues ahead under power, slamming into the forward end and creating the damage reported by divers. The front end sinks in shallow water and stern drives on a bit further before dropping to the bottom. Considering the fracturing in two of the *Carl D. Bradley* in November 1958, and *Daniel J. Morrell* in November 1966, the idea perhaps isn't so far fetched.

The collision theory was largely trashed in 1972 when divers discovered the *Davock* upside down in depths in excess of 215 feet of water, 1.9 miles off Little Sable Point Light, 20 miles south of Ludington and ten miles south of the *Minch* wreck off Pentwater. The divers found no evidence of collision. The rudder, however, was hard over as if she was trying to climb out of the wave trough, a virtual death sentence for her.

The *Anna C. Minch* seems to have been a bit of a "bad luck boat" moving from accident to accident. She started a string of ill fortune in April 1907, when the steamer *Harvey D. Goulder* smacked into her at a grain elevator in Superior. In November 1911, she bounced hard against a dock in Chicago. She struck the end of a bridge protection pier at Lorain in September 1915. During a storm she and the *Theodore H. Wickwire* broke loose from their mooring in Buffalo and struck several other steamers and crushed a yacht in March 1916. In November 1916, she collided with the steamer *Charles M. Warner* in Lake St. Clair receiving major damage to her bow. The *Steel King* rammed her in November 1917, in Toledo and the following February she was hit by the *Mathew Andrews* and *Philip Minich* at her mooring in Cleveland. Her rudder got the worst end of it when she grounded in Lake St. Clair in August 1920, and the *Harry W. Croft* nailed her in Buffalo. The following October she grounded on Bois Blanc Island east of the Straits of Mackinac. She experienced storm damage two months later at Erie, Pennsylvania, and again the following February. She hit bottom twice in Conneaut in October 1923. Her propeller was damaged the next month in Milwaukee. She drove into the dock in Duluth in November 1924. In October 1925, she did the same trick in Buffalo and two months later lost her way in the fog and went up on Fox Point, Wisconsin.

Novadoc

The third ship lost in the Armistice Day storm, the 254-foot Canadian canaller *Novadoc*, was the lucky one, blowing hard up on the shallows south of Pentwater, Michigan, three and a quarter miles, 21 degrees from Little Sable Point light.

Observers ashore could see men huddled in the forward end of the ship even as massive storm waves pounded into her broken hull. It was much like the *Mataafa* in this regard; folks safe on the sandy beach watching the drama unfolding before their sand-stung eyes. Clearly it was a case of rescue the crew or their death was certain.

While she was the luckiest in terms of lives lost, she was also the most notorious tale to emerge from the storm.

The *Novadoc* was built in 1928 by Swan, Hunter & Wisham Richardson, England, New Castle. Owned by Paterson Steamship Limited, she was enroute from Chicago to Port Alfred, Quebec, with a cargo of sulphite coke when snared by the storm.

This overhead photograph clearly shows the Novadoc's *hatch arrangement. Author Collection*

The first part of her trip to Chicago was uneventful with a quiet crossing of Lakes Ontario and Erie. Lake Huron was a different story. High seas forced her to shelter at Harbor Beach, Michigan, for a day and a half until the wind finally blew itself out, and she was able to haul her hook and continue.

Pentwater had a U.S. Life-Saving Service Station since 1887. It was the old Life-Savers who had and lived the motto, "regulations say we have to go out but they say nothing about coming back." The Pentwater crew performed many thrilling rescues, plucking sailors from certain death in the cold and unforgiving lake. But in 1915 the old Life-Saving Service merged with the tax collecting U.S. Revenue Marine emerging as the shiny new U.S. Coast Guard. For a time the Coasties, who were made up of the old Life-Saving crews, in fact still carrying the "rate" of "surfmen," continued a tradition of no holds barred daring do. But over time the old time Life-Savers retired and were sometimes replaced with men far less enamored of risking their own lives for the government's nickel. Now it wasn't everyone, many of the new Coasties reveled in the old traditions and did the very best they could under whatever challenges fate threw at them. However there weren't always enough of them and over time the traditions

NOVEMBER: THE CRUELEST MONTH

The old Pentwater Life-Saving Station was an important link in the Great Lakes rescue coverage. Author Collection

faded and allowed less than capable men to assume command responsibilities. Such was the case in Pentwater in November 1940.

What follows isn't the official Coast Guard version of events but it is what happened as remembered by many townsfolk in Pentwater. Ask the old-timers and this is the story (or a reasonable variation) they remember. The "real" story is more complicated but the outcome was the same.

According to popular lore with a wreck just offshore and men clearly going to die if rescue didn't happen, the local Coast Guard Officer- In- Charge refused to go out! It was too rough, or too cold, or too early in the day, or the boat wasn't polished or engine sputtered sometimes, etc. Justifications are easy to come by when the lake is howling and mountain-high seas pound the shore. To some folks it seemed he managed to find an excuse to condemn honest sailors to the whim of Davy Jone's Locker.[7] A claim was later made since he didn't see any sailors on the wreck why bother to do anything dangerous? The townsfolk waited for a day and a half for the Coast Guard to make the rescue, not to mention the freezing sailors facing death on the wreck.

Fed up with the Coast Guard's lack of action, a local fisherman, Clyde Cross, (author's note - the finder of the *Minch* wreck)

Clyde Cross - hero of the Novadoc. *Author Collection*

announced he was going to take his tug out and check for missing fishing nets. While a ridiculous thing to do in the storm blown waters, he and two crewmen, Joe Fountain and Gustav "Corky" Fisher fired up the 22-year old, 40-foot *Three Brothers II*, the oldest fish tug in town and churned out the harbor and into the still tumultuous lake.

Instead of heading for his nets, Cross swung her over to the stranded *Novadoc* carefully laying her alongside the broken steamer. The shipwrecked sailors quickly piled aboard the wave tossed tug as several hundred eager spectators on the beach cheered. Cross promptly turned his overloaded little tug back for the harbor and soon moored up to his dock, the sailors promptly crowding into a

The tug Three Brothers II *approaching her dock. Author Collection*

Landing the Novadoc *crew. Author Collection*

little fish shack for shelter. An old wood fired stove provided desperate warmth for the near frozen sailors. One man was in such bad shape he was immediately taken to the local hospital at nearby Hart.

The tug didn't emerge unscathed from the rescue. Her starboard bow was holed just above the waterline and later examination showed her skeg and stem were twisted. The hole likely resulted from laying up to the wreck and skeg and stem damage from the violent action of the waves. But she was the little tug that could!

When the Coast Guard realized what happened, that mere fisherman had the effrontery to show them up, rescuing the sailors when they said it was impossible, they promptly marched the entire *Novadoc* crew down to the station and issued the appropriate news release about the heroic rescue, and taking credit for it! To their small thanks the Coast Guard provided the survivors with hot food and it is even rumored, a stiff belt of rum! It was later claimed the Coast Guard was getting ready to go out when Cross, "beat them to it." While it is an interesting excuse, it doesn't account for the days of opportunity missed while the sailors waited in vain for rescue.

At this point the record becomes more official but no less "unusual" or pointed, both in the stated actions and even more important, unstated ones.

After the rescue the survivors were taken to Muskegon, Michigan, by chartered bus for a quick official investigation and then home to

Toronto by train. Their shipwreck adventure was finally over but the controversy continued. Interestingly, none of the crew appeared at a subsequent Coast Guard investigation into the actions of the Pentwater crew.

According to news reports, shortly after the crew arrived ashore Captain Donald Steip of the *Novadoc* reached into his pocket and offered Cross a big wad of bills in payment. Cross refused to accept the money, which didn't surprise the folks in Pentwater. One resident claimed, "He would have gone to the help of those men without the prospect of getting a dime." Later though, his two crewmen took the cash, saying they would evenly divide it. The men knew courage doesn't pay the bills.

All the *Novadoc's* crew were extremely thankful to the fishermen knowing how close they came to death. The First Mate saying, "A sudden shift in the wind would have finished the ship for good. Before we were taken off this morning I would have given the ship two more hours before she broke completely apart".

Unfortunately two of the *Novadoc's* crewmen were already dead. Captain Steip explained his cooks were swept off the stern by a wall of water when they tried to reach the bow while the ship was grounded offshore.

As mentioned previously, Cross's involvement with the storm wasn't finished. When the lake calmed he went out looking for the

The Novadoc *running heavily laden as evidenced by the comparatively low freeboard. Author Collection*

The Novadoc *in the breakers. Author Collection*

wreck of the lost *Minch* and success rewarded his efforts, hard-hat divers confirming his find. The moral of the story seems to be, "if you want something done, give the job to a fisherman."

Interviewed later by a news reporter, the *Novadoc's* mate explained how the *Novadoc* came to end up on the shoals. Caught in the maw of the storm, battered by the mountainous seas and blasts of wind, she was clearly heading for the beach. "We ordered all our boys to put on lifebelts and come to the bridge as we could see that nothing could save the ship. The captain thought if he put the engines in reverse, perhaps we could keep clear... but we were getting closer to the beach. Then all at once the ship was in the backwash from the shore and of her own accord, she turned around, heading out into the lake.

"The captain put the engines full speed ahead. Then things happened so quickly one could scarcely follow them. Several huge waves slammed in the steamer, the shock knocking the crew to the deck and smashing out the pilothouse windows. Everyone received cuts and bruises from the broken glass and wreckage. The captain stopped the engines and just then the ship struck the shoals with a shock that shook her from one end to the other, keeping it up until she was finally banging up against the bank about 500 feet from shore... " She struck about 7:00 p.m. immediately breaking in half and snapping all electric power cables and steam pipes forward.

The sailors fled the bridge to the captain's quarters to get away from the water coming in through the smashed windows. For a while they all took their situation with good humor figuring rescue would eventually come. But the Coast Guard never came.

Seas continued to hammer the steamer. Just before dawn the port side forward door caved in and the crew fled to the captain's office. They prayed the thin wall between office and quarters would hold up since they had nowhere else to flee. When the wall began to weaken they propped it up with boards. Since both lifeboats were long gone, swept off into the inky hell of the storm, the men were totally dependent on help from shore. But the Coast Guard never came.

The seven men in the engine room and cooks aft were in more serious trouble, the booming waves breaking through portholes and flooding their quarters. For a while they bailed with buckets, throwing the water back out the same portholes it came in. But they couldn't keep up and soon everyone was soaked through and standing knee deep in freezing water. By the second day they had enough and decided they had to somehow make their way forward. Timing the waves they dashed to safety in the forward cabins, all making the deadly run except the two cooks, swept to their icy death by a rouge wave rumbling hard down the spar deck.

Another *Novadoc* survivor was wheelsman Lloyd H. Belcher of Victoria Harbor, Ontario. He stated when they were leaving Chicago about 3:00 a.m. and passing the Coast Guard Station, the captain yelled over to the watchman asking if they had a weather report. The Coast Guardsmen said no, so the steamer continued on across the lake. Weather report or not, the *Novadoc* had cargo to deliver.

Belcher later said when he went on duty at noon on the 10th the wind was still southeast but the seas were growing. An hour later the captain told him the barometer had, "gone right to the bottom".

The broken steamer battered by the waves. Author Collection

NOVEMBER: THE CRUELEST MONTH

Since the wind was blowing southeast they crossed the lake to shelter under the Michigan coast before running north to the Manitou Passage and on to the Straits of Mackinac. But when the wind shifted hard southwest at 2:00 p.m. they were in deep trouble since the powerful blasts would slowly but inexorably force them on the beach. They were too far from the west shore to fight their way against the wind and waves to return under its protecting bulk.

Belcher recalled the captain decided to come about and try to ride the storm out further off shore, warning the crew "...to stand by as we were going to turn around and we would likely roll heavy. We turned the wheel hard-a-port and asked for a second ring (author's note, a second ring meant more power) but the ship just laid in the trough of the seas and rolled." With little other choice the captain managed to turn back to his original course, which would in theory just clear Little Sable Point Light.

At this point the men on the steamer had no doubt they were in deep trouble. Huge seas were climbing up the port quarter and flooding aboard. At 6:00 p.m. Belcher was relived at the wheel but decided to stay in the pilothouse to see what would happen. Half an hour later the tarpaulin over number six hatch cover ripped open. The mate took him and another man out on the wild deck and they quickly nailed a plank across the hatch in an effort to reseal the tarp. It was dirty and dangerous work but had to be done.

The captain tried to turn the ship again to head out into the open lake but again he didn't have the power to do it. Wind and wave kept driving the bow back towards the Michigan coast. This time they were too close to land to work back to their original course. They could only hang on and wait for the inevitable collision with the offshore bars.

By now the *Novadoc* was just off Little Sable Point Light and the lightkeeper could see the steamer's masthead lights as she struggled with the storm. He had a front row seat to shipwreck.

Belcher continued his tale (after fetching up in the shallows just off an area known as Jupiter Beach), "About 9:30 in the morning (Monday the 11th) we noticed three men on the shore walking up over the hill so we tried to draw their attention by waving a sheet out the door. At last they saw us so they went back over the hill and about an hour later there were about a dozen men coming down to

Little Sable (Sauble) lighthouse. Built in 1874, it was an important navigation aid for coastal shipping. Author Collection

the shore. During the day the crowd got bigger and soon there were hundreds of people there but no one would dare come out in those raging waters. As we were only 700 feet from shore we tried to shoot a line to the shore but had no success. (Author's note: many ships were equipped with line throwing guns on the order of the famous Lyle gun, Coston, Galbraith and Schuller being popular manufacturers. Usually shipboard line throwing guns were never successfully used since training was invariably a neglected part of shipboard routine. As will be discussed later the Coast Guard strangely never attempted to fire a line to her. A Lyle gun had a range of 400 yards or 1,200 feet. Since the *Novadoc* was only 700 feet offshore it should have been doable.)

Belcher continued, "We kept sending up rockets to let the people on shore know that we were still alive. As darkness came on for the second night we saw that we had no chance of being rescued that day so we all sat around hoping for the best. By this time we were cold and getting quite hungry, as we had nothing to eat for two days. The mate then found a pail and made a little fire in it to warm us up a bit. We broke up the chairs and furniture for wood and when that was all

Commander A.F. Glaza in his Coast Guard uniform in 1920. Note the Gold Life-Saving Medal on his chest. He was as genuine hero of the Coast Guard. Author Collection

gone we started on the walls - we had a little axe with us so we broke up the walls with it. On shore they kept a fire going all the time to try to encourage us and to let us know there was nothing to do but wait until help arrived. During that night the sea had gone down and when daylight came the Captain went down to the after end of the boat to see who all was there. We knew there was someone there as they were throwing water out the porthole. When he came back up forward we found to our sorrow that the two cooks had been washed overboard and that one fireman was almost all in from exposure." (Author's note: there is some question exactly when the cooks were lost.)

When the Coast Guard never came, some of the men became so discouraged they were prepared to try to swim to shore. It was better to try and fail than never try at all! Others dissuaded them from such suicidal efforts.

The Coast Guard eventually convened a special investigation regarding its involvement with the *Novadoc* debacle. Commander Anthony F. Glaza from the Chicago Division office headed-up the investigation. It must have been a difficult assignment for Glaza. He was an authentic Coast Guard hero, awarded the extremely prestigious Gold Life-Saving Medal for his participation in the rescue of the crew of the steamer *L.C. Waldo*, wrecked off Keweenaw Point, Lake Superior during the infamous November 1913 Great Lakes

The broken Waldo *on Gull Rock Reef. The rescue of the crew was one of the most heroic episodes in Life-Saving Service history. Author Collection*

"hurricane" that wrecked 17 ships killing 250 sailors. At the time he was part of the Eagle Harbor Life-Saving Service crew.

Soon after his birth in Bay City, Michigan, in 1892 his family moved to Grand Marais where he became acquainted with the Service first hand. He signed up with the "storm warriors" in 1911 at age 19 and transferred to Eagle Harbor the following year. Standing six-foot three inches tall he was an imposing figure. He later served as Officer-In-Charge at Crisp's Point and Vermilion Point stations. When commissioned as a warrant officer in 1918 he was the youngest officer of his rank in the Coast Guard. In 1926 he was back at Eagle Harbor but now commanding the station. When a powerful November storm accompanied by below zero temperatures slammed into Lake Superior he again faced shipwreck, he and his men rescuing the crews of the steamer's *Thomas Maytham* and *City Of Bangor*. For Glaza, it was always about leadership. Good leaders will get the job done regardless of the difficulty.

Subsequent promotions and transfers sent him to duty in Buffalo, New York, Green Bay, Chicago and Detroit. During World War II he held various important positions, retiring after a 38-year career in 1946.

By any measure Glaza was an old time Life-Saver brought up in a culture of rescue against all odds, perseverance and daring do, to have to investigate the actions of a crew that in the public's eyes, failed to perform to the level expected of them, must have been very distasteful. Regardless of his personal feelings, orders are to be obeyed and Glaza carried on.

Glaza, assisted by another division officer, Commander G.B. Skinner, was careful to tell the press that the, "…district headquarters sought merely to determine whether the Coast Guard had been negligent in its duty. Nobody is on trial." For the purpose of the proceedings Chief Boatswain's Mate Alfred E. Kristofferson in charge of the Ludington Station and Chief Boatswain's Mate Alfred M. Anderson, in charge of the Grand Haven station were named as defendants. Kristofferson was named since he was the senior man present during the wreck.[8] No specific charges were made against him. Under the prevailing Coast Guard organizational arrangement he supervised not only the stations at Ludington and Pentwater but also the Point Sable Lighthouse.

Alred E. Kristofferson was another hero of the Coast Guard, receiving his Gold Medal for the Runnels *rescue.* Author Collection

Like Glaza, Kristofferson was another hero of the Coast Guard, awarded the Gold Life-Saving Medal as the Number one Surfman during the spectacular rescue of the crew of the steamer *H.E. Runnels* at Grand Marais, Michigan, Lake Superior in November 1919. Since the Grand Marais keeper, the legendary Benjamin Truedell was on leave at the time, Kristofferson stepped up to his responsibilities as he was trained to do. In November 1940, Kristofferson was a 29-year veteran and already was involved in 13 major rescues. (See the chapter on the *Owen* wreck for details of the *Runnels* rescue.)

Born in Sweden in 1884, he was fluent not only in his mother tongue but also German. After arriving in America in 1907, he quickly became proficient in English and in 1911, joined the U.S. Life-Saving Service with early assignments to several Chicago stations. When the steamer *Eastland* capsized in the Chicago River in 1915 he played a role in helping haul the living, and later dead, to shore. He gradually rose through the ranks with assignments to numerous Great Lakes stations, several as the Officer-In-Charge. Kristofferson was recognized numerous times for heroism. Besides the Gold Medal for the *Runnels* wreck, he received the bronze medal for heroism during World War I, a Memorial Star from the Coroner of Chicago for the *Eastland* work and Certificates of Recognition from the city of Kenosha, Wisconsin, for his work with wreck of the steamer *Wisconsin* in 1929 and from the Treasury Department for 1938 wreck of the *Ewig*. Like Glaza he knew what rescue was really all about.

The investigation started on Monday, November 25. Point Sable Lightkeeper William B. Krull was the first witness, telling the officers he first sighted the *Novadoc* about 8:00 p.m. on the 11th. He burned flares to warn her off but once she went on the bar he tried to notify Ludington Coast Guard Station but the telephone lines were down. He finally managed to get through to the Muskegon Station, which in turn

The capsizing of the Eastland *in the Chicago River was the worst maritime disaster in Great Lakes history. Author Collection*

contacted the District Headquarters in Chicago. They instructed the keeper to get in his car and drive to Ludington to report the wreck. This he duly did, passing the word to Boatswain's Mate Rouleau since Kristofferson was on scene at the *City Of Flint 32* wreck. Meanwhile Chicago ordered the Muskegon Station to drive to Grand Haven and alert them of the wreck since telephone communications links were also out of service. The duty fell to Boatswain's Mate Raymond G. Chapman. On the way to Grand Haven he stopped at the White River Coast Guard Station and collected additional men. Since he was also at the *Novadoc* wreck site, Glaza asked Chapman about the possibility of rescue. Chapman replied, "a boat would have been smashed in the attempt" and a breeches buoy rescue was "unlikely" due to the waves breaking over the steamer. Pressed by Glaza if he would have done anything different had he been in charge, Chapman said he would have put the beach apparatus in place so they would be ready in the event the steamer started to completely break-up.

Coast Guard Machinist's Mate William F. Barnhart later testified the beach apparatus equipment could have been manhandled from the end of the road over the sand dunes to a point opposite the wreck to be ready for use. Barnhart was a 31-year veteran of the Coast Guard, his career starting back in 1909, when the men of the old Life-

Kristofferson helped recovering victims from the Eastland. *Author Collection*

Saving Service regularly did the impossible hauling breeches buoy gear and surfboats too, by hand, miles over soft sand and wave washed beaches! Clearly an old Life-Saver's view of what could be done differed from those of the "new breed."

Boatswain's Mate Anderson from Grand Haven testified he was notified the night of November 11 by the Muskegon station to take his surfboat and equipment to Little Sable Point where a vessel was in distress. He arrived by truck about 7:00 a.m. on the 12th but saw nothing. After sending a search team consisting of Ernest Pratt and Hector Monroe, both crewmen from the White River Station, north along the beach, he went on to Pentwater Station. It wasn't long though before the call came in the steamer was sighted about a mile north of the point. After arriving on site he determined it was impossible to get his equipment over the dunes to the beach and even if he did and fired a shotline to the steamer, the seas were breaking so hard over the wreck the sailors would never be able to walk the open deck to secure their end of the breeches buoy, saying "if any of the crew had ventured from their haven in the pilothouse it would have been suicide for them." When Kristofferson arrived later in the morning Anderson claimed he agreed with his decision.

Standing high on a dune and looking out at the *Novadoc* with sand whipping in his eyes, Kristofferson later said he was sure he could read her name also stating, "I saw no signs of life aboard; pilothouse and about three or four feet of the hull stuck up above the water forward. Could see hull about two or three feet above water the entire length. The engine house appeared to be partly submerged on the outside. Ice was forming over the vessel." The fact he saw no one on the wreck was likely because by this time the crew was sheltering in the captain's cabin and out of view.

Kristoffersen also told the board, "I told Anderson to take charge as he was the next senior officer present next to myself and advised him to have the boat in readiness to go out as soon as possible. I did not know if there was a living person aboard the *Novadoc*..." At the time Kristofferson's major concern was the *City Of Flint 32* and his need to be onsite to supervise the rescue effort so he quickly returned to his crew at the car ferry.

The car ferry City Of Flint 32 *was Kristofferson's major rescue concern in the 1940 storm. Author Collection*

The City Of Flint, *another victim of the storm. Author Collection*

When questioned if he considered sending the big 36-foot motor lifeboat from Ludington to Pentwater when the seas moderated on the 12th, he replied, "I didn't know there were survivors and having left orders at Pentwater I thought either there had been no survivors or if there were, they were taken off as we had no difficulty navigating our motor surfboat at Ludington on the morning of the 13th." Since telephone lines between Pentwater and Ludington went down on the 11th and weren't restored until the afternoon of the 13th his ability to determine what was (or was not) happening at Pentwater was severely constrained. Mostly he was relying on Anderson to handle the *Novadoc* wreck.

Sending the big boat to Pentwater was to a point problematic. Kristofferson knew he had approximately 50 people aboard the *City Of Flint 32* and if anything went wrong he would desperately need the boat. Since he had no knowledge of anyone alive on the *Novadoc*, his best use of the boat was to keep it on stand-by in Ludington. From his examination of the steamer and given the terrible conditions on the beach, he surmised if anyone was alive on the wreck they were in the pilothouse and sheltered from the wind. "I did not think they would starve and I did not think they would be comfortable but I did think they would survive." In other words he made a command decision in asset allocation.

NOVEMBER: THE CRUELEST MONTH

It is worth noting that since the sailors on the *Novadoc* fired rockets when she went on the bar and their ad hoc sheet distress signal brought a horde of local citizens to the beach the following morning complete with later bonfires, both the lighthouse keeper and Pentwater Coast Guard had to know at least some of the crew were alive. Apparently they (Anderson?) failed to tell Kristofferson thus hampering his decision-making. The failure to send critical information "up the chain" is a problem organizations constantly fight. Commonly it can be traced back to a lack of local leadership and initiative.

When the board asked, "Are you satisfied that Anderson put forth every effort to rescue the men?" Kristofferson gave less than a glowing recommendation stating, "Due to the fact that I was not present, I do not know except by hearsay what was done but I know if I had been here myself, I would have made sure the motors were operating and possibly would have had a boat in the water on the 12th running the motor every hour or two to keep it from freezing so it would be ready for instant service." Whether Kristofferson and Anderson ever worked together before isn't clear. Doubtless Kristofferson trusted him to get the job done, a task he utterly failed to accomplish. Anderson certainly didn't have the same level of wide shipwreck and leadership experience as Kristofferson. As late as 1934 he was only a surfman at the Sheboygan Coast Guard Station.

During the investigation Boatswain's Mate Anderson complained to Glaza about Cross and his tug crew claiming that when the Coast Guardsmen were preparing to launch their boat in Pentwater Lake at 8:00 a.m. on the 13th to go out to the wreck and rescue the sailors, they ended up stuck in the mud. Cross and his tug passed within 100-feet but failed to stop and help them! It took them 20 minutes to free themselves and by that time Cross had already rescued the crew (author's comment - thus robbing Anderson and his men of the glory).

Anderson's tale was certainly self-serving since when Boatswain's Mate Chapman testified earlier he stated when the Coast Guard tried to start the Pentwater boat the engine refused to fire and since there was not one able to fix it, they had to launch the Grand Haven boat, adding to the delay in reaching the wreck. Getting stuck in the mud was just one more problem in a litany of them for Anderson.

Glaza asked Anderson if the *Novadoc* men could have been rescued earlier. Anderson said no, saying, "The skipper of the *Novadoc* told me himself that he was glad we didn't try to shoot a line. He said the men would have interpreted the move as the last and only means of rescue and would have undoubtedly been washed overboard in the attempt."

When Clyde Cross took the stand Glaza was careful to state, "On behalf of district officials and ranking Coast Guard personnel, I want to thank you for a splendid job." Cross explained he spent 12 years as commercial fisherman, ten in Ludington and the last eight months or so out of Pentwater. Contrary to the popular Coast Guard story of keeping a close watch on the wreck from shore, he said when he was on the beach at 1:30 p.m. on the 12th he saw 50-75 civilians but no Coasties. He said the waves were still running too high for a surfboat launch from the beach. Feeling something needed to be done for the poor sailors on the wreck he went to the station and offered his boat but was refused. Asked by Glaza if he felt every effort had been made to get the sailors off the wreck he said, "No, it would have been my way to bring the big boat down from Ludington at midnight Tuesday. It could have stood-by and possibly have taken the men off." To add to the Coast Guard's discomfort, Cross read a letter from the *Novadoc's* Captain Donald Steip. "If it hadn't been for you, all my men would have perished. Am sure your boat was the best one that could have taken us off. I wonder what kind of investigation the Coast Guard is going to have. I don't see what they can find out. It might have exposed them for not being prepared and not going out sooner to try to do some good." (author's note - the captain's letter is in sharp contrast to Anderson's earlier testimony).

Concerning his failure to stop and help the mud trapped Coast Guard, Cross explained he and one of his men were below deck working on his old Buick engine and the third was wheeling her. Given the noise from his engine, he couldn't have heard a call from shore nor seen the stuck boat from below. He said he had no way of knowing the Coast Guard wasn't already at the *Novadoc* but simply went out to look for his nets and if needed, stand-by to assist the steamer. When he saw no one was at the wreck he made the rescue.

Cross's crewman Joe Fountain substantiated the story. When asked if he thought the Coast Guard was negligent he didn't mince words, stating, "I believe the leader was. I believe he could have had a boat launched and ready."

Chief Boatswain's Mate Arthur F. Anderson, normally in charge of the Pentwater station testified he was gone on sick leave when the storm struck on the 11th and didn't return to duty at the station until just before the *Three Brothers II* returned with the survivors.[9]

Compounding the whole mess was a telephone call about 7:00 p.m. on the 12th from Commander Gordon W. McLane, Chief of Staff for the Chicago Coast Guard District to Alfred Anderson at Pentwater. McLane ordering him, "not to be in too much of a hurry and to take no chances imperiling the lives of the survivors on the boat." Given such milk-toast orders what was any self-respecting Coastie to do? Rescue at sea is inherently dangerous. Was Anderson left to think, "The big boss wants me to do nothing and those are orders I can follow."

The Pentwater Station received another call about 6:00 a.m. on the 13th just as the men were sitting down to breakfast. The unidentified caller said he was at Point Sable and urged them to get out to the wreck right away and remove the men. This prompted the belated rescue effort. Why they responded so quickly to this strange telephone call was never explained. Did the caller know Cross was going out to get the sailors and if the Coast Guard wanted to beat him they needed to get moving?

Mr. Leland Kent, Superintendent of the Pere Marquette carferries, testified on the last day of the inquiry. He was bitter over the absence of the Coast Guard Cutter *Escanaba* during the entire storm stating, "it is the command of the *Escanaba* and not the Coast Guard along this shore that should be investigated. That boat looks pretty at yacht races etc. in the summer but in the fall and winter when it is most likely to be needed where is it? In the shipyard at Manitowoc. It has been there so long it is practically taken root! It certainly is the silliest and most asinine thing to send a boat of that caliber to a shipyard in the fall and keep it there for months. I have been in the ship yard three to five times a week and I know the delay was caused by poor judgment."[10][11] He said this wasn't the first time she was taken out of service in the fall. He also defended Kristofferson's presence at the *City Of Flint 32*. His logic was the same as the Coast Guardsman's; 51 known lives at risk versus an unknown number, if any, on the *Novadoc*.

Glaza sent his report "up the chain" and using a large bucket of whitewash reserved for such faux pas, the Coast Guard covered over the entire *Novadoc* debacle. Boatswain's Mate Alfred Anderson, the Non-Commissioned Officer Kristofferson put in charge of the *Novadoc* rescue, was mildly disciplined delaying his promotion to the next higher grade for a year. Kimball must have spun in his grave.[12] Kristofferson certainly did his best in a "no win" situation. Under the circumstances he could only trust Anderson to do his job.

While I have castigated the Pentwater Coast Guard crew for failure to come to the rescue of the *Novadoc*, it clearly is a command problem. Without leadership the crew will fail. Certainly the telephone call from the District Chief of Staff, Commander McLane, ordering that no risks be taken had a chilling effect on rescue operations. But his call came relatively late in the affair. Had Alfred Anderson exercised the leadership the situation required he could have taken a number of actions:

1. Brought the breeches buoy apparatus to the beach opposite the wreck in preparation for possible use. Had the wreck started to literally come apart, the beach apparatus was the only option with any chance of success. But this meant a lot of work hauling it over the dunes.

2. Launched the motor surfboat in Pentwater Lake in preparation for use as needed.

3. Periodically started the surfboat engine to assure it was ready to go at all times.

4. Accepted Cross's offer to take the Coast Guard out to the wreck in the *Three Brothers II*. That Anderson had no specific authority to do so isn't reason not to use it. Figuring out ways to solve problems is called initiative and is critical at every level of command.

It is also crystal clear each and every one of these actions would likely have been taken by any of the old Life-Saving Station keepers. They would never have failed to do everything possible to make the rescue.

It is worth noting the official daily log for the Pentwater Coast Guard Station for November 1940, is missing from the repository in the National Archives and Records Administration. It is assumed it disappeared during the subsequent official investigation. Given things like missing logbooks, it is easy to accept the idea of a whitewash.

Residents from Pentwater and Ludington felt Cross and his crew should be honored for their heroism. On behalf of the citizens the Ludington News submitted an application for Carnegie Hero Fund Awards for Clyde Cross, Joe Fontain and Gustav Fisher. The

The Coast Guard 36-foot motor lifeboat was a superb coastal rescue craft. But it was still a case of iron men in a wood boat! Author Collection

application was supported by letters from Congressman Albert J. Engel and other leading citizens as well as special petitions. Carnegie Hero Awards are very prestigious, often including a cash stipend, but are only given after detailed investigation. Apparently Cross and his crew didn't make the cut which is not surprising considering from it's inception on April 15, 1904, until January 31, 1939, of 38,111 applications only 3,086, or approximately 8 percent were granted! Of the 3,086 awards made, 2,514 were bronze medals, 553 silver and a mere 19 gold! That Cross and his men weren't honored by the Carnegie Hero Fund is in retrospect, not surprising and certainly does not denigrate their heroic actions in rescuing the *Novadoc's* crew.

Regardless of the action of the Carnegie Fund, on Thursday, December 5, the local Board of Trade held a testimonial banquet at the Community Building to honor Cross, Fontain and Fisher. Hundreds of well-wishers gathered to enjoy the venison dinner and program. The three men each made a few remarks and a letter of commendation from Congressman Engel was presented. Other luminaries added their accolades including a speaker representing retired Coast Guardsmen. Given the circumstances, it is a shame his comments were never recorded. It was a great showing of recognition for the three fishermen. Reputedly the Canadian government awarded Cross a medal for his action since the *Novadoc* was a Canadian vessel.[13]

While the Coast Guard certainly received a deserved black eye for their *Novadoc* debacle, elsewhere on the lake crews were working to the finest traditions of the service.

While searching for the missing fish tugs the 36-foot Coast Guard motor lifeboat from Grand Haven fought her way through the storm to Chicago, clear across Lake Michigan. The little wooden lifeboat took the worst the lake could throw at her and kept on going. When she and her four man crew finally made Old Chicago Coast Guard station the boat had burned 180 of her 200 gallons of fuel! Boatswain's Mate Elmer Dudley, a 16-year veteran said, "it was the worst storm on the lake that I have ever seen and I've been in plenty of them." These men did their job bravely and with all the skill of the old Life-Savers. And don't forgot the crew that took their 36-footer out to St. Helena Island to make certain the crew of the steamer *Frank J. Peterson* was safe. They, too, displayed remarkable courage and skill. It is deeds like these as well as the Coast Guardsmen standing by the grounded *City Of Flint 32* that make the abysmal performance of the Pentwater crew so startling.

Approximately 40 shipwrecks litter the cold waters off Pentwater. The *Davock*, *Minch* and *Novadoc* being the most famous. The toll from the three wrecks, *Minch*, *Davock* and *Novadoc* was truly horrible - 67 **sailors** lost to Lake Michigan's Armistice Day storm.

Perhaps the best summary of the whole mess is from Captain Peter Zealand, Fleet captain for the Pickands, Mather fleet owner of the *Davock*. When the Coast Guard investigators asked him for recommendations to prevent similar future losses, he pointedly replied, "The only protection is when you get some place where if you do get caught, the best thing is to check down and ride it out if you can. If you can't we will sit down around a table and try to find out what happened the same way we are doing here. A lot of that is just left to the master of the ship, that is what he is there for, that is his responsibility and we cannot sit at a desk in a nice warm room and tell him what to do when he is out in the lake and the only man that knows exactly what the situation is." It was good advice in 1940 and good advice today!

References:

Ann Arbor News, November 14-15, 1940.

Anna Minch, *William H. Davock*, *Novadoc* Files, Stonehouse Collection.

Annual Report of the Lake Carriers Association 1940.

ARMISTICE DAY STORM, November 11-12, 1940 -

<http://www.crh.noaa.gov/mkx/climate/big.php>

Lloyd Belcher, "Sailor Recalls November 1940 Disaster." *The Nor'Easter, Journal of the Lake Superior Marine Museum Association*, September-October 1991, 1-4.

Dwight Boyer, *Strange Adventures of the Great Lakes*, (Cleveland: Freshwater Press, 1974), 100 -104.

Dana Thomas Bowen, *Memories of the Lakes* (Cleveland: Freshwater Press, 1969), 264-275.

Chicago Daily Tribune, November 10-15, 1940.

Cleveland Plain Dealer, November 10-20, 1940.

Carnegie Hero Fund Commission, *Carnegie Hero Fund*, (Carnegie Hero Fund Commission - Office, 1939), 76. 79-81.

"Daily Log Coast Guard Station Grand Haven, November 10-20, 1940", NARA RG 26.

"Daily Log Coast Guard Station Holland, November 10-20, 1940," NARA RG 26.

"Daily Log Coast Guard Station Ludington, November 10-20, 1940," NARA RG 26.

"Daily Log Coast Guard Station Munising, November 10-20, 1940," NARA RG 26.

Detroit Free Press, November 12-15, 1940.

Detroit Marine Historian, February 1991.

Chief Boatswain (L) A.F. Glaza, "Great Lakes Hazards." Unidentified clipping. 12-15.

Great Lakes Journal, January, June 1941.

George W Hilton, *The Great Lakes Car Ferries* (Berkley, California: Howell-North, 1962), 146-147.

Saralee R. Howard-Filler, "Deliverance," *Michigan History Magazine*, November - December 1981, 30-32.

Lake Fury, Storms of the Century, Special Edition - Safe Ashore, the 1940 Armistice Day Storm, (CD Media) Airworthy Production, LLC.

Ludington Daily News, November - December 1940.

Marine Collection, Rutherford B. Hayes Library.

John M. Mills, *Canadian Coastal and Inland Steam Vessels, 1809-1930*, (Providence, Rhode Island: Steamship Historical Society of America, 1979).

NOVEMBER: THE CRUELEST MONTH

Milwaukee Journal, November - December 1940.

Fred W. Mikko,. "One Day's Rescue Work By Boatswain Anthony Glaza," *Inland Seas*, Fall 1988, 172-175.

Monthly Weather Review, Volume 69, Number 6, June 1941, 169-178.

November Witches Battle Great Lakes - <http://www.usatoday.com/weather/news/1998/wnov1113.htm>

Official Obituary, Commander Anthony F. Glaza, U.S. Coast Guard.

"Pentwater History" - <http://pentwaterhistoricalsociety.org/Information.htm>

John H. Purves, *Roen Steamship Company, The Way It Was 1909-1976*, (John H. Purves, 1983), 29-31.

Runge Collection, Wisconsin Marine Historical Society.

L.C. Sabin, "Commerce on the Lakes," *U.S. Coast Guard*. July 1939.

Scheina, Robert L., *U.S. Coast Guard Cutters and Craft of World War II*, (Annapolis: U.S. Naval Institute Press,1982), pp. 20-21.

"Survivor Recalls Sinking of *Novadoc*", November 11, 1940; <http://www.shipwreckmuseum.com/stories.phtml?artid=53>

S.S. Anna C. Minch - <http://en.wikipedia.org/wiki/SS_Anna_C._Minch>

U.S. Coast Guard, Notes and Documents Relating to Losses of *William H. Davock*, *Anna C. Minch* and *Novadoc*, Stonehouse Collection.

U.S. Coast Guard, Eleventh District, "One Hundred and Forty-Fifth Anniversary Celebration," 1934.

U.S. Department of Commerce, Marine Inspection and Navigation, Notes and Documents Relating Relating to Losses of *William H. Davock*, *Anna C. Minch* and *Novadoc*, Stonehouse Collection

ANNA C. MINCH, WILLIAM D. DAVOCK & NOVADOC

University of Detroit Mercy, Fr. Edward J. Dowling, S.J. Marine Historical Collection - *William H. Davock*.

Reverend Peter Van der Linden, (ed.), *Great Lakes Ships We Remember* (Cleveland: Freshwater Press, 1979), 159, 292, 312.

Washington Star, November 13, 1940.

West Michigan Underwater Preserve Proposal, <http://wmup.org/content/view/12/26/#davock>

Footnotes:

[1] Armistice Day used to mark the anniversary of the symbolic end of World War I on November 11, 1918. It commemorates the formal armistice signed between the Allies (United Kingdom, Commonwealth, France, Belgium, Russia, Italy, Japan and the U.S) and the Triple Entante (Germany, Austria-Hungry, Ottoman Empire and Bulgaria) ceasing hostilities on the Western Front, which took effect at eleven o'clock in the morning - the "eleventh hour of the eleventh day of the eleventh month" of 1918.

The date was declared a national holiday in many of the allied nations recognizing those members of the armed forces who were killed during the war. In the early 1950s people in the U.S. began calling it Veterans' Day in recognition of all Veterans. In 1954 President Dwight D. Eisenhower signed a bill proclaiming November 11th each year as Veterans' Day.

In 1968, a law changed the national commemoration of Veterans' Day to the fourth Monday in October. People rebelled against this blatant congressional buffoonery protesting that November 11th was a date of historical significance. Finally, in 1978, Congress returned the observance to its traditional and proper date.

[2] Reputedly the wreck of the *Indian* was later discovered in the breakers near Port Shelden. One of the bodies of the crew of the *Richard H.* was found just south of Grand Haven by a patrolling Coast Guardsman on Saturday Morning.

[3] Coal was measured in short tons, 2,000 pounds. By contrast iron ore was in long tons of 2,200 pounds.

[4] Her summer marks were 20-foot 2 3/4 inches, intermediate at 10-foot 9 3/4 inches (mid September - November 1) and winter at 19-foot 3 inches.

[5] Her coal consumption is an interesting look into the era of coal fired steamers on the lake. A relatively small ship in 1940 she burned about 245 pounds per mile traveled. By the time she reached Ludington, her last reported position and 670 miles from the coal dock, she would have burned 75-80 tons changing her average mark (between bow and stern) to 18-foot 5 inches, 7 inches above her winter marks. In other words the more bunkers she burned the "safer" she became.

[6] The historical context of the phrase "Chinaman's chance" comes from the old railroad and Goldrush days of pre-California, where many Chinese worked as laborers for the First Transcontinental Railroad. They were often employed for dangerous jobs involving explosives, often for half the pay of the Irish workers. Their survival was often problematic. It essentially means someone has no chance at all of accomplishing an action. There are also numerous variations of this explanation. The original expression was, "Chinaman's chance in hell."

[7] The bottom of the sea; the resting place of drowned mariners.

[8] Some news accounts spell the name Christofferson however Kristofferson is correct.

[9] The two Andersons certainly adds a layer of confusion.

[10] It is worth noting the Coast Guard apparently learned nothing about scheduling major vessel maintenance in the fall. When the *Edmund Fitzgerald* was lost in November 1975 off Whitefish Point, Lake Superior, several major Coast Guard vessels including the icebreaker *Mackinaw* were undergoing scheduled maintenance and unavailable for search and rescue duty.

[11] The *Escanaba* was a 165-foot cutter built by the DeFoe Works in Bay City, Michigan in 1932. She was stationed in Grand Haven from 1932 - 40. With the start of World War II she was sent saltwater and was lost on June 13, 1943 while performing convoy escort in the North Atlantic. Only two of the 110 men aboard survived. It is still

debated whether she fell victim to a German torpedo, struck a mine or suffered an internal explosion.

[12] Sumner Increase Kimball was the General Superintendent of the old U.S. Life-Saving Service. He maintained the highest standards for his crews. Failure to absolutely make the best effort possible to rescue shipwreck victims was cause for instant dismissal. Contrast this with the performance of the Pentwater Coast Guard crew.

[13] In spite of considerable effort, I can't substantiate this claim.

ABOUT THE AUTHOR

Frederick Stonehouse holds a Master of Arts Degree in History from Northern Michigan University, Marquette, Michigan, and has authored many books on Great Lakes maritime history. He is the 2006 recipient of the Association for Great Lakes Maritime History Award for Historic Interpretation and received the 2007 Marine Historical Society of Detroit  Historian of the Year Award. *The Wreck Of The Edmund Fitzgerald; Steel On The Bottom, Great Lakes Shipwrecks; Wood On The Bottom, Great Lakes Shipwrecks; Great Lakes Crime, Murder, Mayhem, Booze And Broads; Great Lakes Crime II, More Murder, Mayhem, Booze And Broads; Great Lakes Lighthouse Tales; Women And The Lakes, Untold Great Lakes Maritime Tales; Women And The Lakes II, More Untold Great Lakes Maritime Tales; Lake Superior's Shipwreck Coast; Went Missing Redux, Unsolved Great Lakes Shipwrecks; Final Passage, True Shipwreck Adventures; My Summer At The Lighthouse, A Boy's Journal* and *Cooking Lighthouse Style, Favorite Recipes From Coast To Coast* are all published by Avery Color Studios, Inc.

He has also been a consultant for both the U.S. National Park Service and Parks Canada, and an "on air" expert for

National Geographic and the History Channel as well as many regional media productions. He has taught Great Lakes Maritime History at Northern Michigan University and is an active consultant for numerous Great Lakes oriented projects and programs. Check www.frederickstonehouse.com for more details.

His articles have been published in numerous publications including *Skin Diver, Wreck and Rescue Journal* and *Lake Superior Magazine*. He is a member of the Board of Directors of the Marquette Maritime Museum and a member of the Board of Directors of the United States Life Saving Service Heritage Association.

Stonehouse resides in Marquette, Michigan.